MW00790418

New Foundations for Psychoanalysis

Jean Laplanche

New Foundations for Psychoanalysis

Translated by David Macey

Basil Blackwell

English translation copyright © Basil Blackwell Ltd 1989

First published as *Nouveaux fondements pour la psychanalyse*, Presses Universitaires de France, 1987

This translation first published 1989

Basil Blackwell Ltd
108 Cowley Road, Oxford, OX4 1JF, UK

Basil Blackwell Inc.
3 Cambridge Center
Cambridge, MA 02142, USA

British Library Cataloguing in Publication Data

A CIP catalogue record for this book is available from the British Library.

Library of Congress Cataloging in Publication Data

Laplanche, Jean.
     [Nouveaux fondements pour la psychanalyse. English]
     New foundations for psychoanalysis/Jean Laplanche: translated by David Macey.
        p. cm.
     Translation of: Nouveaux fondements pour la psychanalyse.
     Bibliography: p.
     Includes index.
     ISBN 0-631-16661-0 — ISBN 0-631-16662-9
(pbk.)
     1. Psychoanalysis. I. Title.
     [DNLM: 1. Psychoanalysis. WM 460 L314n]
     RC504.L35513   1989
     150.19′5—dc19
     DNLM/DLC
     for Library of Congress   89-908
                                                                  CIP

Typeset in 11 on 12½pt Baskerville
by Setrite Typesetters Limited
Printed in Great Britain by Billing & Sons (Worcester) Ltd

Contents

Translator's Note

In common with a number of French psychoanalysts, the author makes a consistent distinction between *pulsion (Trieb*; 'drive') and *instinct (Instinkt)*. That distinction is not always observed by the translators of the *Standard Edition of Freud*, and quotations have been modified accordingly.

It should be noted that the use of the term *baquet* (translated here as 'tub') is in part a reference to the curious equipment used by Mesmer.

Acknowledgement is due to Sigmund Freud Copyrights Ltd, the Institute of Psycho-Analysis and the Hogarth Press for permission to quote from *The Standard Edition of the Complete Psychological Works of Sigmund Freud* translated and edited by James Strachey.

David Macey
Leeds

1
Introduction

New foundations for psychoanalysis? Why the need to go back to
fundamentals, and what justification is there for describing
foundations as 'new'? The need is quite clear to me: the
course I have been teaching at the Université de Paris VII
since 1969 has been published in a series of volumes entitled
Problématiques (Laplanche, 1980a, 1980b, 1980c, 1981, 1987),
and the sub-titles are a clear indication of how matters stand.
My tactic has always been to take an apparently classic
theme in Freudian psychoanalysis, and to call it into
question, challenge it and problematize it. Calling a theme
into question means upsetting things and putting the very
basis of the whole psychoanalytic experience to the test. This
is quite definitely a problematic which privileges the
Freudian experience and which is centred upon Freudian
concepts.

If we call things into question in this radical and violent
way, a new thematic, a new order, and new concepts, or a
new ordering of concepts, necessarily emerge. My views on
instincts, on narcissism, on language, and on many other
themes, are quite clear, but they have been expressed in a
rather disorganized fashion. The moment has come for me to
show how they are articulated, even if it does entail a certain
schematism. That is, perhaps, inevitable, and even as I begin
this account I feel the unfortunate effects of both a need to
cover the 'foundations' theme and a wish to say everything.
Hence the race against time, and an approach which is
which is not the leisurely 'spiral' I have sometimes been able
to follow.

Founding anew

Foundations: laying foundations by making a constant critique of so-called basic concepts means repeating founding gestures and movements; but *what* do they found? They found *psychoanalysis*, and they provide the foundations for *a* psychoanalysis in the sense in which we speak of being in psychoanalysis, and, finally, they found the human being. For, and I stress this point, nothing can found psychoanalysis unless it awakens by its deferred action echoes of something that has a foundational value for human beings.

Foundations, then. But *new* foundations? Whenever the term 'new' crops up, people become suspicious and warning bells begin to ring! I could allude to a recent press report which proclaims (yet again) the demise of psychoanalysis and of its intellectual production, but which ignores some of the richest works to be found in the recent literature. Reports of the demise of psychoanalysis are merely the obverse of an unquenchable thirst for novelties at any cost. Psychoanalysis is expected to be a constant source of novelty, of new thrills. When psychoanalysis, and French psychoanalysis in particular, surrendered to the effects and fascination of fashion — and it did so long ago — it set off down what might, to paraphrase Freud (1900, p. 566), be termed the 'shortest path to fulfilment of the drive', the primary process or even the death drive. When we begin to hunger after thrills at all cost, we allow the death drive to work untrammelled.

Let us be wary of the term 'new', and let us adopt the adage cited by Freud (1926b, p. 193): 'Every step forward is only half as big as it looks at first.' It might be said that this is scepticism. But it is certainly not just any scepticism, as psychoanalysis has its reasons for adopting this adage. Psychoanalysis shows us that history is neither a continuous nor a cumulative process, that it does not have a happy ending, that it does not evolve smoothly and that its course is marked by repression, repetition and the return of the repressed. If, moreover, we refer to an older philosophical tradition — and I am thinking of the tradition of Hegel as well as of the heritage of Heidegger – we see that making a new contribution does not necessarily mean making innovations, that it does not necessarily mean straying away from basics. There is, then, an interplay between the terms 'new' and 'foundations': we are going back to our foundations in order to renew them. Going back to our sources.

I would also like to stress one other point: I am applying the adjective 'new' to 'foundations' and not to 'psychoanalysis'; in my view, there can be no question of a new psychoanalysis. Psychoanalysis exists. It is both a developing situation and a developing practice – which also develops into a theoretical practice, a point to which I shall return – and there can be no question of innovation at all cost, no matter how attractive that may seem in certain quarters. What we have to call into question, renew and explain is that which founds psychoanalysis.

Basic concepts and Freud's epistemology

Making a clear distinction between foundations and practice does not, however, imply that we are faced with an absolute opposition, as it is quite obvious that laying new foundations inevitably has an effect on practice, just as a certain modern shift in practice inevitably influences the way we view our foundations. In insisting that there is, even so, a relationship between foundations and practice I may perhaps be going against what Freud sometimes has to say on this question. I allude in particular to a passage in 'On Narcissism: An Introduction' (Freud 1914, p. 77), but one could find many other remarks in similar vein in which the most general concepts in psychoanalysis are described as being the 'top of the structure', as though they were far removed from experience and were potentially interchangeable. In these passages, Freud makes a deliberate show of being sceptical about speculation, but his scepticism is in complete contradiction with his inspiration and with his deep-seated need to look for basic concepts.

There is also another more nuanced epistemological text which I would like to discuss briefly: the well-known opening passage of 'Instincts and their Vicissitudes' (Freud, 1915a, pp. 117−18), where Freud discusses the need to appeal to a concept as basic as that of 'drive' (my own comments are enclosed within square brackets):

We have often heard it maintained that sciences should be built up on clear and sharply defined basic concepts. In actual fact no science, not even the most exact, begins with such definitions [as we shall see, the whole text describes a *general* epistemological position, and makes no reference to the specific features of the search for basic concepts and of conceptualization *in psychoanalysis*]. The true beginning of scientific activity consists rather in describing phenomena and then in proceeding to group, classify and correlate them [Freud will of course come back to the term 'phenomena'; this is not a blind empiricism]. Even at the stage of description it is not possible to avoid applying certain abstract ideas to the material in hand, ideas derived from somewhere or other but certainly not from the new observations alone [observations require a rough conceptual framework borrowed from somewhere or other, simply because they can be noted, discussed and described]. Such ideas − which will become the basic concepts of the science − are still more indispensable as the material is further worked over. They must at first necessarily possess some degree of indefiniteness; there can be no question of any clear delimitation of their content [the return of clear definitions is very much a secondary consideration and, as we shall see, a stage which is never completed]. So long as they remain in this condition, we come to an understanding about their meaning by making repeated references to the material of observation from which they appear to have been derived, but upon which, in fact, they have been imposed. Thus, strictly speaking, they are in the nature of conventions − although everything depends on their not being arbitrarily chosen but determined by their having significant relations to the empirical material, relations that we seem to sense before we can clearly recognize and demonstrate them [intuition and what we will soon discover to be speculation do, then, have a role to play]. It is only after more thorough investigations of the field of observation that we are able to formulate its basic scientific concepts with increased precision, and progressively so to modify them that they become serviceable and consistent over a wide area. Then, indeed, the time may have come to confine them in definitions. The advance of knowledge, however, does not tolerate any rigidity even in definitions. Physics furnishes an excellent illustration of the way in which even 'basic concepts' that have been established in the form of definitions are constantly being altered in their content.

It is important to note that this paragraph, which, as we have seen, describes a fruitful interplay between observation and concepts, ends with a discussion of *physics*: basic concepts do not exist from the outset but, even at the descriptive stage, there exist vague ideal frameworks which, rather like garments which are not too tight or too restrictive, are both conventional and non-arbitrary, and borrowed from somewhere or other; and the do-it-yourself borrowing by psychoanalysis of concepts from related domains is obviously one of the problems we will have to examine. It is only at a later stage that sciences focus upon basic concepts, and that an attempt is made to delimit and define them; but the definitions are always subject to revision.

Physiology as foundation: the rot sets in

This is all very well, and the text is fine, but, I repeat, it is in no sense specific to the psychoanalytic approach. To be more accurate, it incorporates psychoanalysis into a general epistemology, and gives it the same status as the natural sciences. That is why I cannot resist the temptation to go on to the next paragraph. You will see why. The following paragraph introduces the concept of 'drive', and borrows from physiology, from the physiology of the *Reiz*, which is usually translated as 'excitation', although it might be better rendered as 'stimulus', as distinct from *Erregung* ('excitation').

The concept of 'drive' is, then, to be understood with reference to the broader notion of stimulus. To quote Freud:

> A conventional basic concept of this kind, which at the moment is still somewhat obscure but which is indispensable to us in psychology, is that of a 'drive'. Let us try to give a content to it by approaching it from different angles.
>
> First, from the angle of *physiology*. This has given us the concept of a 'stimulus' and the pattern [and this is where the fun begins, if I may put it that way] of the reflex arc, according to which a stimulus applied to living tissue (nervous substance) *from* the outside is discharged by action *to* the outside.

The notion of a stimulus and the 'pattern of the reflex arc' are supposed, then, to shed light on the concept of the drive. But the pattern, as described by Freud, is, as I have demonstrated again and again, absolutely erroneous: it is a pattern derived from a *false physiology*, or even a puerile physiology. The idea that a stimulus applied to living tissue from the outside remains the same when it emerges from that tissue stems from an elementary and indefensible mechanism. We know that the final muscular discharge has nothing to do with *either* the stimulus energy *or* the nervous energy that is channelled through the 'reflex arc'. Muscular energy, such as the energy which causes a knee-jerk reaction when the patellar tendon is tapped with a hammer, obviously has nothing in common with the energy imparted by the hammer. The whole process is a sequence of trigger reactions, not one in which energy from the outside is transferred and then evacuated. There is nothing in either the receptor extremity or the motor extremity which can be likened to an attempt to reduce an embarrassing level of excitation. Such a 'pattern' does not stand up for a moment in the face of the physiology of Freud's day, not to mention modern physiology. And Freud must have known that.

Here, then, we have the notion of the reflex arc, described by a false pattern elaborated within the framework of an aberrant physiology, being put forward as a model for psychoanalysis! And, indeed, as an extremely useful model in that, erroneous as it may be, there is something in the psychical apparatus that resembles it: anything that is introduced into the psychical apparatus must be rapidly expelled. And so, this so-called borrowing from a related science merely appeals to a fantastic physiology, or even a folk physiology, *just as* hysterical paralysis appeals to a parascientific anatomy in order to mark out its territory.

I would be loath to leave Freud's epistemological 'purple passage' without stressing how the model falls apart, as though under the weight of its internal contradictions, at the point where he attempts to 'apply' it to the concept of 'drive' and to the 'example' of the reflex arc. As in many other texts (cf. Freud, 1911a) which would appear to be grounded in reason and observation if they concerned the natural sciences or even the other 'human sciences', it is in the disconcerting final lines that the rot sets in. The model borrowed from 'biology', or from psychophysiology, is a *false* model. It is as though it signalled a *twofold* heterogeneity; not only is psychoanalysis *unlike* the other sciences in that it does not develop *in the same way* that they develop; its relationship *with* the other sciences may not be comparable to mutual relations between the other sciences.

This text marks, then, a digression but it is very important in that it strikes an *uncanny* note by introducing the question of relations between psychoanalysis and related domains: not only biology, but also linguistics, history, pre-history and many others. We will later have occasion to consider this problem from all sides. Is it possible for psychoanalysis to import or appropriate basic concepts from the outside? But first of all we have to ask if these concepts do really come *from the outside*. And, to raise a different but related question, what is the meaning of the term 'appropriation of a concept' when it is *psychoanalysis which carries out the appropriation* by effecting a movement which is not merely conceptual but *real*, when, to put it simply, it effects a movement which is necessarily based upon introjection?

The four sites of psychoanalytic experience

Foundations for psychoanalysis are, therefore, foundations
for an experience: the *psychoanalytic experience*. Can the psychoanalytic experience be localized? Does this experience
have any one privileged site? If it does have *one* site, we can
immediately say that it lies in psychoanalytic treatment. But
we have still to define precisely why that site is privileged, as
its privileges may have nothing to do with those attaching to
immediate experience, or to the empirical. After all, few
things are less empirical than a psychoanalysis. What is
more, there is more to the psychoanalytic experience than
the experience of psychoanalytic treatment, and we are justified in classifying the sites, and objects, of the psychoanalytic
experience under four headings: clinical psychoanalysis,
export psychoanalysis, theory and history.

The clinical: treatment   The above list, which puts the clinical
on a par with other sites, indicates, then, that there is more
to the psychoanalytic experience than clinical psychoanalysis
even if, as we must, we define 'the clinical' in strict terms as
'clinical treatment'. And nor, *a fortiori*, is clinical psychoanalysis the site of the psychoanalytic experience if, as
happens all too often, we reduce it to what any ψ (as they
would say in mathematics) can take down from any subject
in any circumstances. The inflation of the concept of the
clinical goes hand in hand with its vague and ill-defined
character, and especially with its value as an excuse. It has
become an excuse for not thinking, a weapon to be used
against all thought. Can it be claimed that this is a salutary
empiricism? I would argue that the empiricism of 'the
clinical' has nothing in common with the great English
tradition of empiricism, and that the great empiricists would
certainly not see it as a continuation of their work. In the
name of the 'return to the clinical', an attempt is being made
to make terroristic use of implicit concepts, most of them
based upon common sense or rendered trite by common

sense. I will have occasion to speak of one of the most recent of these concepts, which has become a sort of catch-all category, especially in English and American psychoanalytic psychology; I refer to the concept of interaction, which is now anti-theory's answer to everything. And I could mention many others.

Can it be said that 'clinical thought' is pragmatic thought? To say so is to do the great tradition of pragmatism (defined as an epistemological stance) an injustice, to forget that true pragmatism certainly takes success as a criterion, but that it refers to the sucess of *thought* and not to the possibility of obtaining an immediate material effect, as those would have it — and there are more and more of them in our circles — whose only comment on every lecture and only contribution to any debate is: 'What is the point? What formula can you give me?' They would give anything for a formula that could ward off the anxiety aroused by our all too frequent therapeutic inadequacies. 'My kingdom for a horse.' 'The whole of Freud for a formula!'

There is no need for us to make a new critique of *vulgar* empiricist or pragmatic thought. Freud does that for us in the passage cited earlier: all observations have to be accommodated within conceptual frameworks, or preframeworks, and those frameworks are refined and modified in a dialectical interplay with experience. One might, as I suggested a moment ago, wonder whether Freud's argument isn't a little too close to being an epistemology for all seasons. Is Freud's epistemology, as outlined in this passage, adequate to its object and to the specificity of its object? It is tempting to speak of the specificity of the human object. True. But there again... Is it simply a matter of contrasting the human sciences with the natural sciences? Incorporating the epistemology of psychoanalysis into a general epistemology of the human sciences will not necessarily get us very far.

Before going any further, I think it appropriate to define two of the specificities of clinical psychoanalysis as object. Firstly, the specificity of our experience of treatment. Our experience is grounded within the framework that founds it in accordance with a rule which has in itself a foundational import, as it is known as the 'fundamental rule': the *Grund-regel*, the rule which is fundamental to what happens in treatment. We will turn later to the question of what the rule founds, or founds *anew*, but for the moment I would stress that the foundational nature of treatment goes far beyond anything that can be said about the experimental conditions which necessarily provide the framework for any experimental apparatus in *any* science ('human' or otherwise). It goes far beyond the precept which states that we must take into account the conditions of observation. It is something which claims to found and give a new impetus to a process which awakens echoes of the process which founds human beings.

Its other characteristic, which is not entirely unrelated to the above, is that *the object of psychoanalysis is not the human object in general*. It does not deal with 'man', a concept which can be defined by many other sciences such as psychology, sociology, history or anthropology, but with the human object in so far as it formulates that object and in so far as it gives its own experience a form. It is of course essentially within clinical language that it formulates its experience but, at a deeper level, this is its very life-blood. Any epistemology or theory of psychoanalysis must take account of the very basic fact that the human subject is a theorizing being and a being which theorizes itself, by which I mean that it is a self-theorizing being or, should the term 'theorize' seem too intimidating, a self-symbolizing being. The symbolization which comes to the human subject during treatment, the interpretations or self-interpretations, and the play of interpretation between analyst and analysand, are a re-symboliz-ation based upon earlier symbolizations, upon primary symbolizations, and our search for foundations necessarily involves us in a search for traces of those symbolizations.

Extra-mural psychoanalysis The second site and object of the psychoanalytic experience is what I term 'export psycho-analysis' or 'extra-mural psychoanalysis'. It is well known that I use this term in order to dissociate myself from 'applied psychoanalysis'. That is certainly the most common and most eloquent term. A term which originates in Freud's own day, but which, in so far as it implies the notion of applica-tion, is open to criticism. 'Application' suggests that a methodology and theory are abstracted from a privileged domain, namely that of clinical psychoanalysis, and then almost mechanically applied as they stand to another domain, just as the science an engineer applies when he builds a bridge is ultimately no more than an ingenious extrapolation from the basic concepts of physics or mechanics. This is why I reject the notion of applied psychoanalysis, which makes a mockery of what we know about its function, its role and its importance within the psychoanalytic movement, and above all in Freud's own writings. In the work of Freud, we see both its importance in quantitative terms and its richness. We have only to recall that the Schreber case or the Leonardo case (Freud, 1911b, 1910a), which were so vital to the development of Freud's thought, are examples of extra-clinical or extra-mural psychoanalysis. We have only to think of the socio-anthropological studies, of *Totem and Taboo* (Freud, 1912–13), of *Moses and Monotheism* (Freud, 1939), of the studies of art and religion, which, when taken together, account for such a considerable proportion of Freud's *oeuvre*. This extra-mural thought is by no means a secondary issue for Freud; its findings always derive from its contact with its object. In view of its richness, I have already had occasion to point out, not without a certain irony, how so many people now try to discredit it with an energy equalled only by the enthusiasm with which they pass psychoanalytic judgement – either openly, which is definitely preferable, or surrepti-tiously – on 'the movement', psychoanalytic schools or the 'psychoanalysis' of their 'dear colleagues'.

When psychoanalysis moves away from the clinical context, it does not do so as an afterthought, or to take up side-issues.

It does so in order to encounter *cultural phenomena*. For when psychoanalysis is exported, it is not exported to just anywhere; not everything outside the clinical realm is an object for extra-mural psychoanalysis, and the conditions that pertain to its domains and methods constantly have to be redefined. Within this movement towards 'outside psychoanalysis', I would make a distinction between two aspects, two movements, or two aspects of a single movement. It certainly has its interpretative, theoretical or even speculative side, but it also has its real side, and that has as yet received too little attention. In referring to its real side, I mean that, in works on so-called extra-mural psychoanalysis, *psychoanalysis invades the cultural*, not only as a form of thought or a doctrine, but as a *mode of being*. Psychoanalysis is a broad cultural movement, and in that sense it is the whole of psychoanalysis which becomes extra-mural. In volume III of my *Problématiques* (Laplanche, 1980c), which deals with sublimation, I attempt to outline a possible theory of *modern sublimation*, if I can use such a term, on the basis of the movement which exports psychoanalysis into culture and which means that psychoanalytic man is not simply man as defined by psychoanalysis and as studied by psychoanalysis, but a man who is, henceforth, culturally marked by psychoanalysis.

Theory as experience The third site and object of our experience is theory. To state that theory is a site and object of experience obviously implies a refusal to grant theory any definitive status of its own, either on the grounds that it is a tool (the expression 'conceptual tool' is sometimes used: 'it has to be of some use') or on the grounds that it is, to a greater or lesser extent, a useless scaffolding (and we know that Freud sometimes flirted — that is the only way to put it — with the idea that psychoanalytic concepts are, basically, a hobby). To state that man is a self-theorizing being is, on the other hand, to state that all real theorization is an experiment and an experience which necessarily involves the researcher. The model is of course Freud. I am thinking of such purely theoretical monuments as the *Project* of 1895 (Freud, 1950), chapter 7 of *The Interpretation of Dreams* (Freud, 1900), *Beyond the Pleasure Principle* (Freud, 1920) and of the recently rediscovered text entitled *A Phylogenetic Fantasy: An Overview of the Transference Neuroses* (Freud, 1987). And how can we approach these monuments, except by seeing them as living experiments in analysis? In such texts psychoanalysis is not something which is lived in relation to an extrinsic object; it develops under its own impetus. These experiences and experiments must themselves be analysed. We have to go further than Freud himself could go. We have to go into them in minute detail, even if it does mean taking them apart, breaking them down and then putting them together again.

This, Freud tells us, is speculation. 'What follows is speculation', he writes in *Beyond the Pleasure Principle* (Freud, 1920, p. 24), and a very similar phrase occurs in the *Overview*. He says it almost apologetically, comparing speculation to the freeplay of fantasy, but we know that speculation soon acquires more weight than any experimental reasoning. One thinks in particular of his famous speculations about the death drive, which stem from 'an attempt to follow out an idea consistently, out of curiosity to see where it will lead', from a sort of 'experiment in thought' which gradually 'thickens', in the sense that a mayonnaise thickens, becomes much thicker than a mayonnaise, and finally sets like concrete. We find biological speculations in *Beyond the Pleasure Principle*, anthropological-historical speculations in *Totem and Taboo* and in the *Overview*; for Freud, speculation is a real 'inner experience', to borrow a phrase from another author. It is not devalued if we mobilize it, if we make it mobile, remobilize it, free it from its artificial bonds, or even give it a new valency, provided that we do not thereby reduce it to the dimension of pure illusion (something which is, for some, synonymous with phantasm or fantasy) or, on the other hand, to a set of purely rational arguments.

History as experience   My fourth point, finally, is as follows. The above remarks about theoretical experience are even more applicable to *history* as site and object of experience. I refer to the history of psychoanalysis, and especially the history of Freud and of Freudian thought. We have yet to exhaust the resources of this thought, and it is possible that we will never do so. It is not simply that it is rich, or brilliant, if we prefer to put it that way; it is the site of an experience which, even in its hesitations, its defences, its prejudices and its repetition, reveals the very contours of its object. When I refer to the history of Freudian thought I am not, of course, referring to a historicizing history; I am in no sense Freud's historian, and others are much more competent than me. I use to my own advantage the history written by others, but that is not the point: my starting point is a reflection on the history of Freudian thought. By that I mean neither the official history of that thought nor revisionist history. The official history consists primarily of the history of Freud himself. On more than one occasion, Freud outlines the history of his thought, either in works specifically devoted to that topic or in passages in other works; this is a falsified history and it has to be treated with great caution; *a fortiori* the official history of the great hagiographers, even when they are as competent as Jones. Conversely, when I refer to history I do not mean the revisionist history − anecdotal or otherwise − that we are sometimes now offered on the basis of a few exhumed documents, even though they are in some cases of obvious importance; it is claimed that this more accurate history will gradually replace the falsifications or platitudes of the official version. I am concerned with the history of a thought which owes its entire inspiration to its object or, if we prefer to put it that way, to its drive. What concerns me in the history of this experience is neither the anecdotes nor the peripeteia (the famous suppressions, the famous changes of heart), but a complex dialectic in which we sometimes hear, as the theory evolves, an echo of human evolution, or even an attempt to imitate it.

It would not, I think, be improper to formulate a new-style Haeckel's law (the familiar 'ontogeny as recapitulation of phylogeny') applicable to at least psycho-analytic thought by postulating that 'theoregeny is a recapitulation of ontogeny'. I have already had occasion to demonstrate this in detail with reference to Freud's theory of drives, of which it has to be said that its temporal development reproduces something of the movement which generates drives in human beings.

At other moments, what can only be called repression, defences and uncontrollable repetitions provide an indication of conflict, of discord and of a phase-difference between thought and its object. These acts of repression, these defences — which, like any defence, often destroy much more than they are intended to destroy and do away with whole segments of reality, in this case a whole segment of the reality of thought — include a sort of cataclysm to which we have yet to come to terms, which we have not yet worked through adequately: the cataclysm brought about by the so-called abandoning of the seduction theory.

We are attempting to found psychoanalysis and not to create it. It already exists within these four sites of experience: the clinical, the theoretical, the extra-clinical and the historical. I use the generic term 'theoretical' to refer to these sites in order to make a distinction between them and the 'practical', in the sense that even what is known as clinical psycho-analysis is in fact a certain consideration [*theorein*] of or reflection on its object, for there can be no clinical psycho-analysis in a purely empirical sense. I refer to four sites of experience and experiment [*expérience*], but French has the disadvantage of using a single word to cover at least three terms in German (and other languages). *Expérience* has to cover both *Experiment* (an experimentalism in which the observer is less important than the object) and *Erlebnis*, which translates as 'lived experience' [*expérience vécue*], and which gives the lived experience precedence over its object. Finally, it also covers *Erfahrung*, which is what I understand

by experience [*expérience*], namely a movement which brings
us into contact with an object and into contact with the
movement of that object.

Founding therefore means founding anew, and founding
anew means going back to the founding act and, of course, to
the founder, namely Freud. What is that founding act? The
act which inaugurates the psychoanalytic situation in the
years 1890−5, and which I call 'the tub' [*le baquet*]. Some
time ago, I began to depict it by means of a schema which
shows that it is both curiously closed (in the sense that a
circle is closed) and open (in the sense that it is tangential to
another circle; that of needs an adaptation; cf. Laplanche,
1980a, pp. 178ff., and especially Laplanche, 1987).

Freud makes an inaugural gesture, but he never seems to
suspect that it has a foundational import only because it
repeats that other founding gesture − or gestures − which
delimits a domain for the human being within the infantile
human being. Founding always means founding anew.

What does this imply in relation to what is known, and
has been known for some time, as the 'return to Freud'?
Countless styles have emerged in the wake of the movement
inspired by Jacques Lacan. What does the return to Freud
mean? Being an orthodox Freudian? And what might that
mean? Or does it, on the other hand, mean putting words
into Freud's mouth, as does in fact happen with certain
forms of Lacanianism? Does it also mean having recourse to
Freud? I refer to the possibility of an apologetic recourse, to
the possibility of playing off certain passages against others.
It will be objected that this means 'Freudian scholastics'. Let
us not exaggerate; Freudian scholastics has never taken on
the dimensions of Aristotelean scholastics or even, to come
closer to home, Marxian scholastics. Rather than a return to
Freud or 'recourse to Freud', I would prefer to speak of *going
back over* Freud, as it is impossible to return to Freud without
working on him, without making him the object of work. We
have to work on his works and, as I have explained elsewhere, we have to put his works to work. And that work calls
his works into question.

2
Catharsis

How, to begin with, does Freud pose the question of foundations? And how, one might also ask, is it posed in later developments, notably in the Lacanian adventure? From the outset it is posed by having recourse to more or less adjacent scientific domains. I will try to examine four examples: the recourse to biology, the recourse to the prehistory of the human race, the recourse to mechanism and the recourse to linguistics. The first three, by which I mean biologism, prehistoricism and mechanism, are constantly bound up with one another in Freud; the fourth is bound up with the attempt to find another 'pilot science', to use an expression which was, for a time, used to connote linguistics in the structuralist milieu.

2.1 Biology

The biological is present throughout Freud. I have discussed this issue on several occasions; for certain of my arguments the reader is referred to my *Problématiques I*, and particularly to the chapter on *'L'Angoisse dans la topique'* (Laplanche, 1980a, pp. 153—250). The biological takes three forms in Freudian thought: it is both an *origin* and a *model* (with all the polyvalency that can be ascribed to that term; I will return to this point in a moment), and, finally, it is a *hope*, a hope for the future in the very specific sense that it offers new therapeutic possibilities.

Biology as hope

Freud never abandoned the hope that a biological, chemotherapeutic method of treating the neuroses would one day replace the psychotherapeutic method and that it would give much more rapid results. This hope is not without its theoretical foundations, and those foundations relate to a specific idea which can be expressed in a variety of ways.

To begin with the chemical nature of the libido. Freud sees libido as the product of a metabolism which is susceptible to discharge and to accumulation and which can therefore have toxic effects. According to Freud, libido is a single substance found in both sexes.

The theory of the chemical nature of the libido is bound up with the old theory of the actual neuroses, which are considered to have no psychological origin or significance but to be determined by a disturbance within the sexual metabolism, by a disruption of mechanisms which would otherwise produce a normal discharge of libido. The theory of the actual neuroses, which is always present and which is never abandoned, indicates, on the one hand, that Freud postulates that a category of actual neuroses exists alongside the category of psychoneuroses, which do have a psychical determination and significance. The acutal neuroses, in contrast, are completely determined by a somatic mechanism, and that mechanism is present or 'actual' as the body is, by definition, a *res extensa* and therefore always exists in the present. But acutal neurosis is, at the same time, more than a limited category: Freud postulates that it is intrinsic to the psychoneuroses in the sense that any psychoneurosis − even on that can be fully explained in terms of psychical factors − comprises a moment of 'actuality', a moment in which it is actualized in the actutality of the body. Indeed that may be the most important moment of all in terms of symptom-formation. This idea is all too often forgotten, but it is rediscovered from time to time. It has, for example, recently been rediscovered in connection with anxiety, as disscussed at the recent conference devoted to that topic.[1] The press, however, reported its rediscovery in very curious terms by establishing an opposition between Freud's position, which was described as being purely phylogenetic, and what might be termed a 'metabolic' theory. The fact that the metabolic or 'toxic' theory of anxiety was Freud's discovery was simply over-looked. In its simplest form the psychogenetic theory (and it can take a simplistic and therefore unacceptable form) sees anxiety as a fear which reproduces an earlier fear; according to the 'actual' theory, the ego is swamped or overwhelmed by an excess of libido. Without wishing to dwell upon the possibility of synthesizing these two points of view, it is worth pointing out that a psychoanalytic theory of anxiety cannot afford to ignore the fact that the body itself is attacked from within by the libido.[2] Similarly, it should be recalled that a general theory of affect can no more avoid the need to take account of the body than can a theory of anxiety — the affects *par excellence*. The modification of the body and of bodily perception is an essential part of the lived experience of affect, so much so that it is neither scandalous nor anti-psychoanalytic to recall that drugs can completely alter that experience, or to formulate a project for its selective and controlled modificaiton.

Biology as model

After this all too rapid summary of the notion of biology as 'hope', I will now turn to the main point I wish to raise and stress in relation to Freud: biology as 'prototype'. The term *Vorbild* is frequently used by Freud, and it refers simultane-ously to a number of ideas. A *Vorbild* is an image, a working drawing or a preliminary sketch; it is both an abstract 'model' and an 'early model' or in other words a 'prototype'. Freud uses this notion on more than one occasion, notably in connection with what he calls the normal prototypes of pathological affections. Mourning, for example, is said to be the normal *Vorbild* of melancholia, and sleep the normal model, or rather the actual model, of the foetal state. But it is

clear from this last proposition of Freud's, which is drawn
from the 'Metapsychological Supplement to the Theory of
Dreams' (Freud, 1917, p. 222) that we might well ask which
is the model and which is the pathological affection. Is the
model something which helps us to understand the affection,
or is it something which comes before it in chronological
terms? If we state that sleep is the normal model for narcissism, we suggest that sleep is the way in which we accede to
foetal narcissism but, according to Freud at least, it is foetal
narcissism which is the prototype for sleep. In a word, which
is the 'abstract' model and which is the prototype (defined as
that which comes first, as in the German *Vor-bild*)? To what
extent does the model describe an origin? And what origin
does it describe? Does it exist within the model, or is it an
external origin?

Given that we are discussing the notion of 'model' (a term
which, I repeat, is not really used by Freud in the sense in
which a more modern epistemology would understand it; the
closest equivalent is the term 'fiction'), let me rapidly point
out that we can identify at least two types of model in Freud
(cf. Laplanche, 1987, pp. 31ff.). On the one hand, we find
'memory trace' models or models of a free process of circulation which might be compared with our modern computer
models. The most famous of these models is that to be found
in chapter VII of *The Interpretation of Dreams* (Freud, 1900),
but we also have a whole section of the *Project* (Freud, 1950).
The famous model in chapter VII describes the successive
reinscription of a sequence of memory-traces. Then there is
another type of model; the 'level' models. These are much
closer to biology, as they introduce the fiction of an *organism*
— and not simply a psychical *apparatus* — which strives to
maintain a certain level, a homeostasis. The two types of
model often complement one another. They can also be
combined, as in the *Project* in particular, where we start off
with a memory-trace model but are soon forced to introduce
the notion of a level which has to be maintained because of
what Freud (1950, p. 301) calls the 'exigencies of life' (the

point being that we act under an intellectual compulsion, *just as* the organism acts under compulsion at the level of its very being).

Biological origins ...

Let us briefly compare the terms *origins, model* and *foundation*, as applied to the biological. The term 'origins' presupposes anteriority. We start out from the obvious fact that we are living beings before we become human beings or 'cultural' beings. No one will dispute this obvious fact: the history of life is such that non-cultural beings existed before culturally marked beings: it is also unlikely that anyone will dispute that fact that, in the history of the hominids, the cultural stage was grafted on to a more biological stage. And finally, it is not unreasonable to assume that the 'anteriority' hypothesis also applies to the development of the individual, as observation allows us to at least reconstruct the existence of an adaptational–non adaptational stratum (so to speak) of neonate behaviour which is not marked by social interaction. So much for the term 'biological origins', in the sense that the hypothesis that the living is prior or anterior to the cultural does not, in may view, mean making excessive demands or concessions.

Let us now look at the question of 'biological models'. Psychoanalysis provides so-called biological models of our human evolution by appealing to the general notion of a living being which is confronted with an environment. Moreover, these are not merely static models; they are working models, genetic models which claim to show how a living being evolves from a simple stage to a more complex stage via a process of differentiation.

Why is it that these three aspects — the anteriority of the living biological element within us, the living being as model for the psyche and the evolutionary or constructive model (which constructs a living being in that, abstract though it may be, it does relate to a living being) — do not result in total confusion as to the respective roles of origins, models and foundations? I am prepared to accept that the biological exists prior to the human. What we have to describe is how the biological-as-model invades the human psyche. This, if I may be permitted to say so, is what Freud sometimes tries to do, notably in connection with the 'ego'.

... But not foundations

Matters are more dubious when it is claimed that the biological presides over the genesis of the human psyche because it provides a living foundation, or in other words that the biological presides over relations between the psyche and life, that the emergence of the human psyche itself is governed by the biological. We have, then, two obvious facts (the precession of the biological and the presence of a biological model within the psyche) and one dubious conclusion (that the very evolution of human psyche is governed by a biological law). And yet the idea that the evolutionary process that leads from biology to the human psyche is *in itself* biological, or even a process of adaptation, implies the theory that the human being is gradually structured as increasingly sophisticated levels of adaptation emerge, due allowance being made for breaks. That theory is widely, even commonly, accepted and rarely challenged.

Some decades ago, this theory — which may now seem somewhat dated — found its expression in the organodynamism championed by Henri Ey (Ey and Rouart, 1938). Ey's theory implied an overall vision of psychopathology, and referred to two sources which were considerd to be compatible: Jackson and Freud. Jackson's theses on the gradual integration of different levels, on the progression from simple to complex, from automatic to voluntary, were combined with the idea of a possible disintegration, of a process of psychopathological breakdown which reproduced the same stages in reverse order. What Henri Ey himself called his 'neo-Jacksonism' was nothing less than an attempt to integrate into this schema the unconscious and instinctual dynamism, which were defined as the first stage in the sequence. And Freud certainly lends himself to this project in more than one sense. A whole line of thought, and a whole series of texts, can be read in this way. It is in texts such as 'Formulations on the Two Principles of Mental Functioning' (Freud, 1911a) that Freud goes furthest in the attempt to contruct the human being as a living substance which evolves from simple to complex and which adapts to the exigencies of life. It is rare for these texts, which have to be described as being inspired by naturalism, not to contain what I term a 'call to order', just as a corner of a dream often contains an index or a 'determinant' which tells us to 'get a grip on ourselves', by saying, for example, that the entire content of the dream must be seen as absurd or contradictory. In this text, the warning shot comes in the penultimate paragraph. Whereas the entire paper centres on the gradual adaptation of an organism to the world, and therefore to reality, this paragraph contradicts the rest of the text by reminding us that the currency of reality (the term 'currency' is Freud's), or the currency of physical reality is not in use in psycho-analysis which is simply not concerned with the domain of adaptation or biological life.[3]

The question appears, to put it another way, to be as follows: does the term 'the biological' have the *same* meaning when it refers to the origins of life or to the concrete organism of the young human being − and I obviously agree that we have to take that into account − *and* when it refers to a model within the psyche, to the living substance we find in the psyche? Freud asks himself this very question in the famous note added to the text (Freud, 1911a, pp. 219−20n.). He himself raises the main objection: the organization he is describing is, as we know, reputedly able to hallucinate the fulfilment of its needs; it lives in a state of autarky, like a monad which is a slave to the 'pleasure principle', and neglects the reality of the external world. Yet such an organiz-ation could not keep itself alive for a moment, and so could not have come into existence at all. But, adds Freud (in remarkably offhand fashion), 'The employment of a fiction like this is, however, justified when one considers that the infant — provided one includes with it the care it receives from its mother — does almost realize a psychical system of this kind.' Freud himself is not, then, unaware of the difference between his 'model', which is, it has to be said, extremely simple and abstract, and a living human being, particularly if that human being is a newborn infant and, in order to reduce the considerable difference between the two, he makes the care infant receives from its mother *part of the model*. But surely the biological model falls apart if it is expanded to include outside intervention, particularly if that intervention is extremely complex and irreducible to being a supplementary element in a so-called autarkic equilibrium?[4]

The Biological model in the apparatus of the soul

Freud does not normally deign to give a more explicit answer to questions pertaining to the concrete living being known as the young human being. He does not in fact see life as beginning with the observable human being; he traces its origins back to what might be called a primitive model, an elementary biological model: the protista, or living matter reduced to its most basic expression. This is, of course, the famous model used in *Beyond the Pleasure Principle*, where Freud refers to an 'animalcule' (1920, p. 47). I have discussed this point at length elsewhere (Laplanche, 1980a, p. 187), and here I would simply like to recall the main points of my earlier arguments. How is this model, which we can call biological, to be characterized? By the fact that it is a 'level' apparatus, to use the distinction outlined above between 'memory-trace' and 'level' apparatuses. A level apparatus is primarily an energetic apparatus which controls quantities of energy and, more importantly, differences between quantities of energy; the function and sole aim of the apparatus in controlling such differences is to preserve its own existence and that, in its own terms, means keeping its level constant. This is what is known as homeostasis and the principle of homeostasis. It would be a mistake to believe that, in a state of homeostasis, the energy level is higher inside the animalcule than it is outside; on the contrary, what the original organism strives to keep constant (in a fiction that we simply have to accept) is a level which is lower than that of its surroundings; the object of the limit is to preserve an internal level of energy that is incommensurate with the energies outside it, which Freud regards as being extremely violent and capable of destroying it at any moment. To take a model of a different, but not unrelated, kind: the purpose of a vase or a glass may be to keep the surrounding environment, but if an empty glass is gently submerged beneath the surface of the water, its function will then be to maintain a level of energy lower than that of its surrounding environment.

A 'constant level' necessarily implies a surface, a limit or something which can maintain it. And in Freud's model, that implies a surface differentiation which maintains a difference of level: as we know, this is what Freud calls the *Reizschutz*, the shield against stimuli. According to Freud, this hardened protective layer is comparable with the cellular membrane of a unicellular organism, and it normally has a twofold func-tion: it protects the energy level, and lowers or reduces the quantity of energy flowing into the organism. Finally, this envelope has a vital role – and this time it is not a funtction – in anything pathological. If it is breached by the inflowing external energy the result will be pain or trauma, as the case may be.

To complete the picture, it will be recalled that surface differentiation results, according to Freud, in the formation of not one but two surface layers: a protective layer and a perceptive layer or the so-called 'perception-consciousness layer' which lies directly beneath the protective layer.

This, then, is what we call a model. How does it relate to the phenomenon? What model and what phenomenon?

Reading Freud, it is very difficult to get a clear picture of what he is trying to depict, as he is probably trying to do several things at once. On the one hand, this is primarily a biological model of an *organism*. That it is a model for all organisms and not merely a model of protozoa is obvious from the explanatory value Freud ascribes to it; it allows him to account for a phenomenon as universal as that of pain: as we know, he regards physical pain as the result of the protective shield having been broken through in a limited area (1920, p. 30). On the other hand, this is also, and I stress this point, a *theoretical* organism, whose relationship with the concrete neonatal organism is rather more than hypothetical, as the mother has to be part of it if model and reality are, more or less, to coincide!

At a second level (and we will find at least three levels), this is a model of a specialized system within a living being and not of the whole living organism; we can refer to this system as the central nervous system or, to use psycho-analytic terminology, the psychical apparatus or the apparatus of the soul [*seelischer Apparat*] but the choice of terminology has certain implications. It sometimes seems that 'central nervous system' and 'psychical apparatus' are roughly equivalent notions, but they have very different explanatory functions: in the case of the central nervous system, it is physical trauma that has to be explained, but in the case of the psychical apparatus we are dealing with psychical trauma. There are certainly analogies between the two, but there is also a major solution of continuity or a vital difference in that, far from complementing one another or being extensions of one another, physical trauma and psychic trauma are mutually exclusive. To put it in very concrete terms, this means that in a traumatic situation the fact of being somatically injured is a way of avoiding psychical trauma and not a way of reproducing it.

We noted a moment ago that the mark of contradiction often appears in the margins of Freud's texts. In *Beyond the Pleasure Principle* we find one such mark in an 'absurdity', though I am obviously not picking up this point simply in order to accuse Freud of talking nonsense. I am alluding to the famous passage in which Freud attempts to find support for his idea that the 'system' develops through peripheral differentiation and especially that the perception-consciousness system lies immediately below the protective layer. Freud attempts to find proof for this assertion in the neuro-anatomical thesis that the cortex, or the seat of consciousness, lies on the surface of the brain. This is obviously an almost puerile thesis based upon an equally puerile macroscopic anatomy, as it presupposes that external stimuli pass directly through the cranium to the cortex. But we know from neuronal anatomy that the cerebral cortex, far from being the first apparatus in the nervous system to be exposed to stimuli, lies right at the end of the afferent nerves.[5] It is so obviously absurd to draw a topographical comparison between the cranium and the cortex on the one hand, and the shield against stimuli and the perception-consciousness system on the other, that it is quite pointless to criticize Freud for doing so. We have to see this as a *sign* of something else, of, that is, the *pseudo-biology* which I am trying to flush from Freud's models in the sense that one flushes a partridge.

Having discussed the organism level and the central nervous system/psychical apparatus level, we now come to the model's final level: that of the *ego*. It is not irrelevant to point out that *Beyond the Pleasure Principle* is the text in which Freud effectively reintroduces the notion of the ego, and picks up a much earlier line of argument. That line of argument originates in the *Project* of 1895 and it still has similar implications. Freud obviously does not equate the ego with the whole of the personality; it is an organ within the personality. But, and this is its second characteristic, it is not just any organ; it is an organism, an organization whose workings are governed by the 'level' principle we defined earlier. Like the animalcule we were just discussing, the ego itself is suspended in the middle of a world of traumatizing energies: the drives.

The vital does not mean Au Fond de l'homme, cela

As soon as we begin to consider this last level — that of the ego — we find that the vital, or the biological, no longer functions as a foundation, in the sense of an actual existing foundation, but as a model and, moreover, as a *real* model, as something which is represented, or causes itself to be represented, within the psyche. That the existence within the human being of a vital level is a presupposition cannot be denied. But, and this is where the problems arise, do we therefore have to say that it is the result of primal repression or that it is the deepest element in the psyche? Yet that is a thesis which runs through the whole of Freud's work and especially throughout a certain Freudian vulgate: the vital is the repressed, and the cultural is both a superstructure and the agent of repression. We find this thesis in both the 'topographies'. In the first, it is expressed in this way: everything which is conscious must first have been unconscious. According to this thesis, the unconscious is simply part of a primordial unconscious domain and its continued existence is the result of segregation. Hence the famous image of the nature reserve (Freud, 1916–17, p. 372) and the reference to Yellowstone, the first national park in the United States (Freud, 1911a, p. 222n.): the unconscious is similar to a nature reserve which is fenced off and therefore kept in its primal state. The best illustration of how this supposed priority of the vital finds expression in the second topography is provided by the title which was suggested for the French translation of Groddeck's *The Book of the It* (1935): *Au fond de l'homme, cela* (In the Depths of Man: It) The id or the it is certainly the lair of something strange and alien; the very term signifies that it is a neutral thing that exists in the thrid person. But does that necessarily mean that the id, the seat of the most obscure drives, and especially of the death drive, is the most biological element within us? That inference is certainly open to challenge. Is the id something primordial and primal, or does it *become* a stranger who lives within us as a result of the very process which constitutes the psychic apparatus and of repression? Does the gesture of separation come before the result of separation? Or does it *establish* the element it separates off?

2.2 Phylogenesis

I would now like to examine the second form of the 'primal' in Freud. I refer to his attempt to find foundations in what might be called phylogenesis or the prehistory or archaic history of humanity.

Once again, the drives are central to the debate. First of all, it should be recalled that Freud's terminology is very clear on this point; despite all the variations introduced by his translators, we find two distinct terms which refer to two very different things: *Trieb*, which we can rightly translate as 'drive', and *Instinkt* ('instinct'). Indeed, Freud usually uses the expression 'instinct in animals' in a very specific sense to refer to a programmed type of behaviour which is fixed and preadapted to a goal, to precisely what the ethologists described at one time as a fixed action pattern.

Instincts lost

There is, however, a certain dialectic between instinct and drive.[6] The whole theme of the *Three Essays on the Theory of Sexuality* (Freud, 1905) could be summarized as 'instincts lost' and 'instincts regained'. The whole point is to show that human beings have lost their instincts, especially their sexual instinct and, more specifically still, their instinct to reproduce. The thesis of the first two sections of the *Three Essays* at least is that human instincts have no fixed or definite object, and no goal, and that they follow no one, stereotypical path. With its descriptions of the sexual aberrations or perversions, which can be defined in terms of both object and goal, the text is an eloquent argument in favour of the view that drives and forms of behaviour are plastic, mobile and interchangeable. About all, it foregrounds their *Vertretungsfähigkeit*, or vicariousness, the ability of one drive to take the place of another, and the possibility of a perverse drive taking the place of a non-perverse drive, or vice versa. The 'instincts regained' aspect of the *Three Essays* can be seen in its account of the transformations of puberty [*die Umgestaltungen der Pubetät*]. This theme might be termed 'instincts mimicked' or 'instincts replaced'. In a complex process of development, they are replaced by something which does, oddly enough, look like an instinctual level. Although it is apparently natural, the genesis of a wish to have a baby is, in Freud's description, far from simple. A woman has to struggle through a veritable labyrinth before she learns to *wish* for something that any living creature instinctively *wants*.

'Instincts regained' is, then, simply the result of a complex and random process of evolution based upon reversals and identifications, many of them bizarre. I am thinking particularly of the phenomenon of identification, which, for Freud, essentially means identification with a love object, so much so that the assumption of a gender implies that the child must first feel a strong homosexual love, a love for the parent of the same sex with whom it must succeed in identifying (cf. Laplanche, 1980a, pp. 341ff.).

Primal fantasies are not innate

Whilst it can be demonstrated that the sexual evolution of the individual is always complex, and that it is not preshaped — or that if it is preshaped, it is misshapen ... — Freud never loses his passionate interest in the preshaped or hereditary element in human beings. The most extreme example of this return of the hereditary is the theory of 'primal fantasies'. If, states Freud (1915b, p. 195; 1918b, p. 120n.), there is anything in man analogous to 'instinct in animals', it is to be found in 'primal fantasies'. In a little text which has recently been republished in book form, Pontalis and I (Laplanche and Pontalis, 1968) exhumed these primal fantasies and established a place for Freud's passion for the phylogenetic. I will exploit the opportunity offered by the republication of the text to distance myself from that notion: reconstructing a body of thought does not mean that one is in complete agreement with its content.

For Freud, primal fantasies are, as it were, a priori categories; they are not simply concepts, but veritable scenarios, and they are four in number: the seduction scenario, the castration scenario, the primal scene scenario and, perhaps, the scenario of the return to the mother's breast. Freud insists that these categories, like any Kantian category, are stronger than the individual's lived experience; if that experience does not conform to the category, it is called to order by the primal fantasy which frames, fleshes out, reorients or even remodels its individual peculiarities.

Freud's prehistoric fantasies

The primal fantasy thesis goes hand in hand with the thesis of the almost endogenous development of the Oedipus, which reaches a crisis point and then declines or is dissolved. And finally, the thesis is completed by the broad prehistoric frescoes which depict primaeval man [*Urmensch*] or the primal horde [*Urhorde*]. In *Totem and Taboo* (Freud, 1912–13), the entire course of the lived experience of the individual is prefigured in a vast prehistoric panorama which depicts how there was once a horde dominated by a powerful father who castrated his sons, made them impotent, kept them under his complete domination, and who laid down the first two laws: the taboo an murdering the father and the taboo on incest with the mother. We know, however, that the primal father was finally deposed by his sons and that they then created a very different type of society: the so-called fraternal society which was dominated by the homosexual bond between the brothers. The sequel to the great saga of *Totem and Taboo* is now to be found in

the recently rediscovered text known as *A Phylogenetic Fantasy.
Overview of the Transference Neuroses* (Freud, 1987). This text, or
draft rather, is written in an almost telegraphic style and dates
from 1915. Freud sent it to Ferenczi, and that in itself may have
influenced the content, as we know that there is a considerable
strand of metahistorical and even metacosmological speculation in Ferenczi's thought. The *Overview* is in a sense a
companion piece to *Totem and Taboo*, particularly in that it
introduces the hypothesis of a pre-horde stage (if we can put it
that way) that exists before the reign of the father. Freud openly
compares it with the primaeval paradise in which there was no
penury, as opposed to the next stage, in which necessity is the
factor that results in the formation of a horde under the
domination, but also the protection, of an all-powerful father or
lord. In the various texts, and especially in the *Overview*, all this
is of course described as pure fantasy, or even as speculation, a
term whose importance has already been noted above. This is
how Freud (1987, p. 11) introduces his account of phylogenesis:

> [I] hope the reader, who for no reason other than boredom
> over many sections has noticed how everything has been built
> on very careful and arduous observation, will be patient if
> once in a while criticism retreats in the fact of fantasy and
> unconfirmed things are presented, merely because they are
> stimulating and open up distant vistas.

Basically, a stimulating balance has to be struck between the
boredom of theory and a clinical knowledge based upon
arduous observation, and the momentary recreation afforded
by fantasy. But this type of fantasy is regarded as fertile and
stimulating, and it often gradually hardens into a tenacious
belief.

The second part of the text begins with a discussion of the
predisposition to neurosis and with an attempt to establish a
concordance between three sets of phenomena. They can be
represented by means of the following schema:

dcba/abcd
ABCD

The series of lower-case letters on the right reflects the appearance of the different neuroses in the history of the individual; the various neuroses normally appear at more or less specific ages, so much so that a certain sequence can be established: anxiety hysteria, conversion hysteria, obsessional neurosis, *dementia praecox*, and so on. On the left, we have a series of events which predispose the individual to neurosis. It will be seen that it inverts the first series: the later the development of the psychoneurosis, the earlier the causal event. In theory, *dementia praecox* is a post-adolescent development, but the events that give rise to it took place much earlier. Finally, and this is both of greater interest to us and more innovatory (if more debatable), we have a sequence of upper-case letters: these indicate a sequence of psychoneuroses affecting humanity in its entirety. It will be noted that here the predisposition to neurosis follows the sequence of the appearance of the psychoneuroses in the individual, and does not invert it. We can see now just how far what has to be termed Freud's passion for phylogenesis can go. It is not only the prototypical scenarios of normality that are preinscribed; so too are the transindividual and metahistorical schemata of the whole of psychopathology. What is more, they follow a historical chronology which reproduces, within a contemporary population, the various ages at which the psychoneuroses appear.

Neither Darwin nor Lamarck

How does what I have termed Freud's passion for phylogenesis relate to theories of evolution? It would probably be a mistake to force it into some broad category. It is well know that Freud proclaims Darwinism to be a vital moment in the history of human thought, that he sees it as one of the three great revolutions which destroyed man's anthropocen-

trism, the others being the Copernican revolution,[7] which
ousted the earth from its central position and the Freudian
revolution, which ousts the human soul from its central role
by showing that it is eccentric to the unconscious. Darwinism
is, then, proclaimed by Freud to be the great doctrine of
evolution, and to claim that a certain latent Lamarckianism
can be detected in this kind of phylogenetic fantasy would
mean jumping to conclusions. To put it in a nutshell, with
Darwin we have random variations or mutations which are
perpetuated by the elimination of the weakest as a species
evolves. With Lamarck we have a struggle with and adaptation to what is assumed to be a primal environment. As a
result, the species acquires modifications which are adapted
to ends and then inherited. We also know that, on the whole,
Lamarckianism has been rejected in favour of a somewhat
generalized neo-Darwinism.[8] But we do not really find either
theory in Freud. He certainly accepts that characteristics
which were 'acquired' over a long period of time were inherited in the course of the existence — or existences — of
historic or prehistoric man. This hypothesis is taken suf-
ficiently seriously and literally, and not in some 'mythical'
sense, for us to be able to wonder if he does believe that
acquired characteristics are inherited. But Freud's acquired
characteristics are very different to those of 'Lamarckian
man', so much so that the term 'acquired' itself is deceptive;
on the one hand, the inherited element does not really relate
to adaptation, thought it may have done so at some point. It
may, for instance, be a neurosis. On the other hand, and this
is more important, the phylogenetic heritage does not consist
of characteristics or of improvements to an apparatus, but of
scenarios which live on in a sort of *memory*; as I stressed
earlier, primal fantasies my flesh out the individual's
memory, and they are situated at the level of memory, not
the level of function. For Freud, it is the history of the
individual which provides the model for human history.
Acquired characteristics are stored away like memories, or at
least *schemata for memories*.

No hereditary memories of scenes

My own position, given that I have to spell it out, particularly in relation to the Laplanche – Pontalis opuscule on 'primal fantasies', is that once we forget that a primal childhood is traced or delineated in childhood memories, we inevitably fall back upon the notion of a genetic heritage of scenes. Let me make myself quite clear: in terms of the somewhat dated debate over the acquired and the hereditary, there can be no question of completely dismissing the notion of predisposition. In using terms like *Anlage* (disposition) and *Veranlagnung* (talents), Freud quite rightly stresses the importance of innate, congenital or even constitutional factors. It is not a matter of deciding between what is innate and what is acquired, but of situating what might be innate: it might be a characteristic which has been acquired by the species, or, using 'innate' in a rather different sense, a predisposition characteristic of the particular genetic line which produced a determinate individual. The acquired characteristics of the human race, or its inborn patterns, are more important than we have been willing to admit. It is also conceivable that there might be constitutional elements in many other domains and that they are specific to particular genetic lines, and therefore to individuals descended from them; one thinks of the sensori-motor ability to adapt, of predominant senses, of the dominance of one or another sensorium which might, for example, be related to one or another type of artistic predisposition; one also thinks of the heigthened sensitivity of some zone in the body to stimulation, of how it can have a natural appeal for a drive which attaches itself to it and becomes stronger. We can also speak, in general terms, of a greater or lesser degree of congenital suseptibility to trauma. On the other hand, the idea of biologically inscribed *mnenomic* scenarios has to be viewed with profound scepticism, and it is probably not acceptable to geneticists, unless, of course, we confuse memory (which is always bound up with instinctual representatives, and behavioural schemata.

The secondary position of 'primal fantasies'

It cannot, however, be denied that, with his primal fantasies,
Freud does discover something prototypical, something
which does go beyond individual experience and which
informs, or even modifies, particular experiences. But that
does not resolve the question of the nature of the 'prototypical'; to be more accurate, there are two questions to be
resolved. How are these fantasies transmitted and where, in
topographical terms, are they located? How are we to locate
these prototypical scenarios within the psychical system of
human beings? Which are they closest to: the id, the ego, or
the super-ego? To take the example of the castration fantasy,
which is probably the deepest of all the primal fantasies.
How can we fail to be struck by the fact that what Freud
now calls a primal fantasy is what he initially discovered to
be one of the sexual theories of children (Freud, 1908)? And
what can that latter notion mean, if not that it is not something which does not well up from the instinctual level, if not
that it is something which is, on the contrary, responsible for
controlling and damning up the archaic element in the
drives. But the drives also raise questions, in every sense of
the term and, no matter whether we call it a theory, a
fantasy or a primal fantasy, *castration* is primarily an *answer*
and not an instinctive question. It is an answer to one of the
many agonizing questions young children ask: what is the
origin of the difference between the sexes? The theory that
explains the difference between the sexes arises because
human beings are theorizing and self-theorizing beings. The
notion of castration is inseparable from the great category of
removal (and ultimately this is a logical category), and the
idea of having one's genitals cut off is — as we can see
from, for example, the history of the species or from prehistoric paintings, (cf. Laplanche, 1980b, pp. 213 —14) — a
secondary idea if ever there was one. It is bound up with the
idea of logical negation (presence — absence, the exclusion of
the third party), and it will, as it happens, help to establish

that idea. The fantasy or theory that castration lies at the origin of sexual difference introduces the human subject to the infinite possibilities offered by the logic of contradiction, but it also imprisons it in a binary logic. If we locate this theory in some primordial unconscious we inevitably blind ourselves to one of psychoanalysis's great discoveries, namely the discovery that the unconscious is characterized by the absence of negation. If symbolic negation is a phenomenon typical of the 'highest' level of the psychical apparatus, why cannot the same be said of castration, which is the fundamental realization of negation? It must therefore be related to the immensely important cultural discovery which introduces the human being to the idea of contradiction.

And, to return to the link we established between the topographical position of the primal fantasy and the problem of its transmission, let us say that the 'secondary' topographical location of the castration scenario suggests that it is a secondary logical pattern which is inherent in verbal communication.

2.3 Mechanism

My third comment on the attempt to find exogenous foundations for psychoanalysis will take the form of a brief discussion of the problem of *mechanism*. Mechanism is one of Freud's basic inspirations, and it is usually explained in biographical terms by relating it to the influence of the 'physicalist' school and to the famous oath which bound together the little clan made up of Brücke, Dubois-Reymond, Helmholtz and a few others. The oath of the physicalists, the text of which will be found in Jones (1954, p. 45), obliges them to ignore everything in psychology that cannot be reduced to the sciences of physics and chemistry. But it goes on to say that, in the event of it being impossible to detect physical and chemical forces directly, it is necessary to 'assume new forces equal in dignity to the chemical-physical forces inherent in matter, reducible to the forces of attraction and repulsion'. Alongside the abstract temptation to reduce the whole of psychology to physics and chemistry, we find a very different and more interesting idea: if it proves impossible — or too long a process — to reduce everything to the physical-chemical level, a physicalist *model* should be introduced into psychology. This brings us back to the second kind of model we described earlier: this is a memory-trace model or even a machine model. And so we come to Freud's mechanical and machine models, the most fully developed example being that given in the *Project* of 1895. Let me rapidly outline those of its features which are most relevant to our purposes.

The physicalist model: four characteristics

First of all, everything is reduced to *figure* and *force*: forces circulate within a spatial model of figures. The figures then take on the more complex form of memory, which is merely the effect of force upon figure; we know that the traces left by the force of the excitation produce 'facilitations', which are simply the physical aspect of what we call memory. And this first point certainly takes us back to a very old tradition that dates back to Descartes at least, and to the duality of figure and movement, as they used to say in the seventeenth century.

My second point is this: this is a *non-biological* model, a non-living model, or even a model *which could not survive for a moment*. It is a model which, from the outset, is open on all sides, as its sole goal is to rid itself of the energy that has been introduced into it.

Thirdly, this mechanism *predates* the biological; the biological simply makes it more complicated. Freud (1950, p. 297) now refers to the intervention of the 'exigencies of life' the *Not des Lebens* which, in some unexplained fashion, intervenes like a veritable *Deus ex machina*, forcing the apparatus to economize on energy, whereas its sole purpose was originally to accumulate energy. By some mysterious means, a non-living machine learns to live or to accumulate energy ... in order to rid itself of energy with greater efficiency.

The fourth characteristic is that this mechanism provides the prototype for the primary psychical process; the latter is of course characterized by the free circulation of energy. The primary process appears before the secondary process, just as life is assumed, in this fantastic genesis, to appear *after* the mechanism. Similarly, the secondary mental process, which does not flow freely, comes after free energy. The free precedes the bound, death precedes life and, as Freud notes on other occasions, notably in *Beyond the Pleasure Principle* (1920, p. 38), 'inanimate things existed before living ones'.

The true model of the id ...

This model raises at least two questions. Firstly, we have to ask the same question that we asked with respect to the vesicle in *Beyond the Pleasure Principle*: what is it a model of? Is it a model of a living being and of its central nervous system? As I have just noted, there is something paradoxical about attempting to teach something to live when it is designed not to live, but simply to be a machine for expelling energy. But if this is not a model of something which exists from the outset, could it be a model of something buried in the depths of the psyche? I insist, therefore on the continued need to stress a distinction which goes against a whole trend — perhaps even the dominant trend — in Freudian thought and to recall that 'original' and 'deepest' are not synonymous. The mechanical element, which exists in the form of a neutral third person, in the form of the id, is in my view the deepest element within the human being, but it is not the starting point.

... *A false physics*

My second question may be of only minor interest to a
psychoanalyst, but it is still irrelevant: what kind of physics
is this? It is post-Cartesian physics, but is it not very dated,
or at least a pre-quantum and pre-relativist physics, a
physics which is still concerned with macroscopic appearances, and which is definitely out of date at the very moment
when Freud tries to press it into service? If that is the case,
the origins of psychoanalysis do not, in epistemological
terms, lie in an innovatory moment in the history of physics,
but in a sort of late flowering. They are lit by the dying
members of a mechanism which may have more to do with
philosophy than with science in any real sense of the word.

What, ultimately, are the elements in play? Is this the
matter described by modern physics? Or is it, as a more
popular view would have it, a matter which coincides in
some way with a certain Cartesianism? Do we have to admit
that psychoanalysis contains other irreducible elements,
other atoms which cannot be split? But we can see that the
transition that leads from such irreducibles as the neurones
of the *Project* to such irreducibles as Freud's ideational representatives or linguistic signifiers is not entirely arbitrary.
Which brings us a fourth set of possible foundations. Once
more, they are foundations extrinsic to psychoanalysis:
linguistics.

2.4 Linguistics

Given that it is impossible to derive the human unconscious
from a living substance which adapts to its environment, the
'linguistic foundations', project attempts to relate it to
something which is both obviously specifically human and
basic to analytic treatment: language. This is of course
Lacan's project, and I have already had occasion to discuss
it at length (Laplanche, 1981, pp. 7–144). On that occasion

I explicitly challenged the canonical Lacanian formula which states that 'the unconscious is structured like a language'.

What linguistics? What language? And what Lacanianism, given that it can take more than one form? The first thing that has to be said, and I have been saying it since 1961, is that if we identify the deepest stratum in man,[9] namely the unconscious, with verbal language (or what we call language in the strict sense), we adopt an explicitly anti-Freudian stance. Not that language does not play a vital role in Freud; we find adequate proof of that in a text such as 'The Claims of Psychoanalysis to Scientific Interest', where the section on the claims of psychoanalysis to the interest of the non-psychological sciences begins with a discussion of its philological interest. I cannot resist the temptation to cite the first lines (Freud, 1913, p. 176.), which give a very clear picture of what Freud understands by language:

> I shall no doubt be overstepping common linguistic usage in postulating an interest in psychoanalysis on the part of philologists, that is of experts in *speech* [those who are concerned with the *logos*, with discourse]. For in what follows, 'speech' must be understood not merely to mean the expression of thought in words but to include the speech of gesture and every other method, such, for instance, as writing, by which mental activity can be expressed.

At the beginning of what is in fact a very dense passage, Freud indicates, then, that language has to be taken to mean both the verbal and the non-verbal.

The secondary situation of verbal language

Verbal language, this time defined in the strict sense of the term, also plays an essential role in Freud. I refer to the well-known discussion of word-presentations [*Wortvorstellung*]. In no sense do word-presentations lie at the root or the origin of the unconscious; for Freud, verbal language is secondary in every sense of the term, in *precisely* the sense that, as we have just seen, castration is situated at a secondary level. Verbal language is secondary in *historical* terms: in terms of the history of the individual, it is perfectly appropriate to speak of a pre-verbal stage. Freud even claims to make use of chronology to detect in the symptomatology of certain neuroses, namely conversion hysteria, a regression to a prelinguistic stage which is characterized by the fact that the distinction between conscious and unconscious does not yet exist. Secondary states such as hysterical hypnoid states, in which the boundary between conscious and unconscious becomes blurred, therefore mark a regression towards a pre-linguistic stage. According to Freud (1916–17, p. 167), language is also secondary in terms of the chronology of collective history, as we can see from his heavy reliance on Hans Sperber's paper (Sperber, 1912) on the sexual origins of the original sounds of speech and language.

Language is also secondary in *topographical terms*: it is a characteristic of the preconscious and of the ego in the sense that it is language that supplies the word-presentations which allow chains of thought to become conscious. For Freud, there can be no conciousness without actual perception. Consciousness is primarily a perceptive consciousness (the consciousness that we possess when we are aware of the world), but we do of course have to take secondary consciousness into account too. This is our consciousness of the content of the psyche, of the content of thought or of memories. Even so, this 'secondary' consciousness is still a matter of perception; it implies that we can put a name to successive and discontinuous flashes of perception, and those flashes of perception, which allow us to become conscious of the content of the psyche, imply the reproduction of word-presentations. It is only because there are points at which we can pin a few words to the content of consciousness, and because we can reactualize, reperceive and revive those words in a real sense, or even pronounce them inside our heads, that it is possible to arrive at a secondary level of consciousness. This is obviously very important for the dynamics of analytic treatment in that it is possible to arrive at a secondary level of consciousness. This is obviously very important for the dynamics of analytic treatment in that it is governed completely by the crucial formula (Freud, 1915b, p. 201) which states that the preconscious presentation is a word-presentation *plus* the presentation of the thing belonging to it.

Verbal language is, finally, also secondary in *economic terms*. It is, in other words, governed by a mode of association and circulation which involves barriers and dams. If thought is to exist, there must be barriers to put an end to an otherwise endless process of circulation. And that is a characteristic of verbal language.

A certain current within Lacanian psychoanalysis, perhaps even the dominant current, tends to locate verbal language at the foundations of the unconscious, which therefore becomes, almost by definition, a transindividual unconscious; although it is obviously very different to the Jungian unconscious, we have here a sort of collective unconscious. The corollary is that verbal language, which is said to be the language of the unconscious, has to function in accordance with the primary process. We are all only too familiar with the mania for outrageous puns which still rages in so many texts by Lacanians old and new, perhaps to an even greater extent than in Lacan's own texts, and which has been denounced in hûmoristic terms as the *yau d'poêle effect* (George, 1979).[10] Because it is centred upon verbal language, this form of Lacanian theory obviously makes it possible for the analyst to listen in a way which has nothing to do with listening to an individual analysand; it privileges the universal, or transindividual if we wish to put it that way, effects of language.

To attempt to make a survey of Lacanianism here, or even a survey of Lacanian views on language, would be to attempt the impossible. Lacanianism is a complex system of thought, and it may perhaps be contradictory when it comes to the question of the verbal and the non-verbal. It is also a system of thought which has evolved considerably. There was a time when Lacan extoled the role of linguistics as a 'guiding science' (this was the heyday of structuralism), but fortunately he later came to realize that a psychoanalytic linguistics would be very different to what linguists understand by the term linguistics.

For my own part, I would say that the most positive element in all this psychoanalytic fuss over linguistics[11] relates to the *signifier*. The notion of the signifier is, of course, borrowed from Saussure, in so far as it is both complementary and opposed to the signified. There *must* also be a further borrowing from Saussure in that the argument is extended away from verbal language: Saussure's foregrounding of the formula for the sign does not lead to a linguistics but to a general semiology or a science of all signifier-signified systems.

The primacy of the signifier; or the signifier designified

Lacan goes far beyond Saussure by asserting that the signifier is independent, or even that it takes *primacy* over any signified. At such points Lacan comes close to lapsing into metaphysics, and a veritable idealism of the signifier raises its head. It may be this which proves so attractive to writers such as Juranville (1984). The more productive side to Lacan's use of the notion of the signifier is, in my view, to be found in the episodic but vital distinction he makes between its two aspects: it is both a signifier *of* (the signified, or so it is implied), and a signifier *to*. What comes to the fore at certain moments is that aspect of the signifier which signifies to someone, which interpellates someone, in the sense that we can speak of an official signifying a court decision, or issuing a distraint order or prefectoral decree. This foregrounding of 'signifying to' is extremely important, as a signifier can signify *to* without its addressee necessarily knowing *what* it signifies. We know *that* it signifies, but not *what* it signifies. A signifier has a discernible significance, and a signifying or significant power; we know that *there is 'a signifying'* somewhere, but there is not necessarily any explicit signified. Lacan suggests the image of hieroglyphs in the desert, or of cuneiform characters carved on a tablet of stone; we know that they signify, and that, as such, they have their own kind of existence, an existence which is phenomenologically different to that of things; they are intended to signify something to us, but we do not necessarily have a signified which we can ascribe to them. This does not imply that we have to agree with the doctrine of the primacy of the signifier or, *a fortiori*, with the doctrine of the hegemony of the signifier or even the hegemony of the signifier in analytic treatment. It simply means that we have to place considerable stress on the possibility that the signifier may be *designified*, or lose what it signifies, without thereby losing its power to signify *to*. I am referring here to the non-verbal signifier as well as the verbal signifier, and in doing so I am beginning to outline the theory of what I call the enigmatic signifier.

2.5 Morphisms

As we come to the end of this brief survey of the heterogeneous and exogenous foundations that have been proposed for psychoanalysis − biology, anthropology or socialanthropology, mechanism and linguistics − we obviously have to concede that all these domains do have a place in the field opened up by psychoanalysis. It might even be said, as I suggested earlier in relation to biology, that their place is twofold: on the one hand they exist on the *boundaries* of the psychoanalytic field; on the other, they exist *within* the psychoanalytic field. But what is the relationship between these two positions? What I want to question is the view that there is a causal relationship at work here. There is a profound difference between what lies on the boundaries of the psychoanalytic field and what lies within it. The relationship between inside and outside therefore becomes one of mutual misrecognition, so much so that psychoanalysis has to rely upon a *false* biology if it is to represent life within the psychical apparatus. In order to make myself understood I will raise yet again what has been termed *the question of anthropomorphism* in psychoanalysis and the critique of that anthropomorphism.

The question of anthropomorphism

Criticisms of the anthropomorphism of, say, Freudian or Kleinian psychoanalysis are based upon the ideal of constructing a scientific rather than a magical psychology. There is, by definition, an element of magic in anthropomorphism; external phenomena are reproduced with the psychological domain so as to promote the impression that psychology can control them. The major reproach addressed to Freud is that human figures are present in the psychical apparatus, and that he cannot do without them. In the first topography, we find the famous image — and it is more than an image — used to describe the censor who stands at the intersection between two systems: a watchman allows certain mental impulses to enter the drawing-room, but not others, admits some and rejects others (Freud, 1916−17, p. 429). The anthropomorphism of the second topography is even more strongly pronounced, as it is assumed that, with the possible exception of the id, the agencies — the ego, the super-ego and especially the ideal agencies — are modelled on human beings who act out human relations on an internal stage in accordance with inter-human scenarios. The masochistic relationship between the ego and the super-ego is one such example. The obvious objection is of course that Freud speaks in the mode of 'as if', whereas the ideal of science is to find a language which does not have to use that mode. The only way to parry that objection is to ask whether human beings might not be constructed in an 'as if' mode. What if

'as if' were not merely a stylistic device to be used at the level
of interpretation ('You are behaving as if the mother inside
you were someone who could make absolute prohibitions');
what if human beings really were constructed in the 'as if'
mode? What if all personalities, and not only 'as if' personalities were constructed in that mode?

There is one other objection which has, I think, rarely
been formulated. It is, however, of crucial importance and
has to be recognized as legitimate. These internalized figures
are not persons; does the *Traumdeutung's* censor, who is part
of the psychical apparatus, have a psychical apparatus? Does
he have an unconscious? At this point we come up against
the limitations of anthropomorphism: these human forms or
'morphisms' are imagos of ourselves, and imagos have
neither a psychical apparatus nor an unconscious. Imagos
have no depth and no transcendance. The same questions
and objections can be raised with respect to the myths of
prehistory. Human evolution is assumed to begin with the
prehistoric father. The formation of a psychical apparatus,
its agencies, its prohibitions and its unconscious, are also
assumed to originate with him. Did that pre-Oedipal father
'have' an 'Oedipus', an unconscious and so on? The answer
lies in the question itself; mythical characters, like those on
the inner stage, are anthropomorphic; they have no depth
and, of course, no historical consistency.

The apparently external foundations that have been proposed for ¯psychoanalysis — anthropology, biology and
mechanism — are therefore both located on the boundaries of
the psychoananlytic and represented within it in the highly
specific form of what might be termed 'morphisms'. Ultimately, anthropomorphism is a false anthropology or a false
social anthropology which has been internalized; it is of
course an anthropology of representation, but that formula is
inadequate, as psychoanalysis cannot be reduced to the
problem of representation, unless we also introduce the term
'unconscious': we can then speak of an anthropology of
unconscious representation.

Biomorphism

Similarly, in terms of the life sciences, we could speak of a biomorphism (if I may be permitted the neologism). In its topographical-energetic description of the apparatus of the soul,[12] psychoanalysis uses *apparently* biological concepts such as excitation, which may even be quantifiable, reflex, organism, or even internal organization (the ego is not simply a structure, and it comprises sub-structures), and the constancy principle. The most obvious example is the complex system of ego-agencies and ideal agencies which keeps the ego in a state of homeostasis. In terms of modern biology, these are false concepts, or at best very rudimentary concepts. The ego is said to be a sac or an amoeba, but that image is far removed from the complex homeostatic mechanisms which govern the human organism. The ego is likened to a substance that lives inside the individual, but it is a rudimentary living substance or even a false image of a living substance; it is something which remains constant in the face of something that metaphorically transforms internal attacks (those that come from the drives) into external attacks.

However, there is an underlying explanation for the internalization of this false biology; in an organism like a small child, which is initially unviable, the vital element must be vicariously represented and supplemented. It is a truism to say that human beings will kill themselves, or might at least be willing to die, for an ideal. A more psychoanalytic observer would note that, if human beings are to live, and not merely die, they need to be loved; they need a *raison d'être*, and their *raison d'être* is love, or the life drive which Freud calls Eros. We must love if we are to live; we must love others, but we must also love ourselves if we are to have any autonomous life, if we are to be spared something of the vicissitudes of loving others. But there is nothing obvious about loving oneself; there must first be a self, an 'ego', as Freud puts it, and so, after a relative eclipse (a very relative eclipse), the notion of the ego reappears in 'On Narcissism: An Introduction' (Freud, 1914). When it does reappear, a new dimension comes explicitly to the fore: it is no longer a central, inhibiting organism, as it once was, but a sort of protoplasmic vesicle filled with love. Its energy level, difficult as it may be to conceive, is love: it is a love-object, and it is only because it is loved that it can love; it is a love-object for the individual, for his erotic drives.

If the individual is to love himself, love life and love in order to live, there must be a living being or a being made in the image of a living substance. The phrase I first cited so long ago ('The ego ... is not merely a surface entity, but is itself the projection of a surface', Freud, 1923, p. 26) is a good introduction to this new notion of the ego: it is not merely a differentiated organ which exists on the surface of the psychical apparatus; it is in itself an internal projection of a 'surface'. What is this surface that is projected within us? It is both our own corporeal envelope, and the surface of the other, the corporeal envelope of the human other. Didier Anzieu has developed this point with great talent, and with numerous clinical examples, in his writings on the 'skin ego' (1985, 1986). This surface is a skin, the skin of the ego, and it originates in the skin of the other. But if that skin should be missing, anything can be used as a substitute skin; as Anzieu demonstrates, words, themselves can be used as a skin.

Life and death 'in psychoanalysis'

As we are dealing with the vital element in human beings, I may perhaps be permitted to make some comments about the title of one of my first books. I refer to *Life and Death in Psychoanalysis* (Laplanche, 1976), in which I took my first steps along the road I am still following. The very title itself introduces at least three sets of questions. What becomes of life and death, in the sense in which we understand those terms in everyday life, in a psychoanalysis? Can one live and die psychoanalytically, in the sense that one can live and die religiously? Isn't that what analysts do? And finally, do not the terms life and death undergo a profound mutation in psychoanalysis? Do they not refer to something very different to what they mean in everyday life? I have already made this point with respect to life. Life in psychoanalysis is not real life. It is neither real everyday life nor life as understood by the biologist; it is an ideal, simplified image of a living substance, and, as Lacan stresses, it can be very alienating. Fortunately, however, it is not simply a matter of alienation. And death? What could 'death in psychoanalysis' possibly mean? As we know, Freud gives two very different answers. On the one hand, there is no unconscious idea of death; there is no need to dwell on that answer as it is perfectly in keeping with the thesis that the unconscious is characterized by the absence of negation. We can make matters even more explicit by showing that, the reason why there is no unconscious idea of death is quite simply that there are *no ideas in the unconscious*, that there is no room within it for negativity, which is a characteristic of all ideas, and especially of the idea of death. At the opposite extreme, we have the notion of what is known as the death drive. The death drive implies a very specific notion of death: its model is neither the suffering and passing away which we are so familiar, nor the decay of the body, and it has nothing to do with the problems that may be posed for us by our 'being toward death'. It relates to a sort of *death before life*, to the so-called inanimate state of matter, to something akin to the silence of death in Pascal's 'infinite space', or to the silence of the surface of the moon. Given the cosmological vision of *Beyond the Pleasure Principle*, this thesis is, in energetic terms, somewhat dubious, as it goes against all the conjectures of the cosmologist by making the tendency towards the equalization of energy come before the appearance of the differences that are bound up with life, whereas it is more logical to think of the universe as moving towards a state of energetic equilibrium rather than away from it. In Freud's cosmological vision, death does indeed

mean the death of mechanism, or in other words the death of
the mechanistic image of a dead machine. Thanks to a
further paradox, death can be said to lie at the origin of a
frantic dionysiac attempt to return to a state of inertia, it is
true to say that in *Beyond the Pleasure Principle* the death drive
appears almost to be the universal principle behind all
drives, the drive which strives to return directly to the
instinctual goal *par excellence*, and to take the shortest path to
the so-called Nirvana state irrespective of how much damage
it may do.

Mechano-morphism

We will come back to the question of the death drive and the
life drive at a later stage of this discussion of the 'foundations' of psychoanalysis; for the moment, let us simply ask
whether there might not be a sort of thanatomorphism in
human beings, just as there is an anthropomorphism and a
biomorphism, and whether it might not be as distorted as
they are. Even so, I would prefer to speak provisionally of a
sort of 'mechano-morphism' in order to define a certain level
within the workings of the apparatus of the soul. I refer to
the primary process, which is one of the great discoveries of
psychoanalysis. The discovery was made primarily in connection with dreams, but there are many other manifestations of the primary process, notably symptoms.

What does it mean to speak of a 'primary' process, putting
the term 'primary' in inverted commas for the moment (a
decision which is subject to review)? It means that there is a
level at which thoughts behave like things, like moving
bodies which transmit 100 per cent of their quota of movement. Displacement in dreams is precisely the same: when
the process of displacement is in full sway, everything moves
from image A to image B or from B to A and no residue is
left behind. Similarly, a whole meaning can be displaced on
to a symptom; the consistency of the symptom is such that it
does not need to refer to anything else and that it evokes, a

priori, nothing but itself; it is precisely that which allows it to
remain so silent, to remain so completely non-elucidated
until such time as the analysis begins. In condensation,
which is the other mechanism of the primary process, an
ideational representative becomes fascinating and pregnant
with meaning because it fuses the energy which is displaced
on to it from two other representatives (displacement and
condensation are complementary, there can be no condensation without displacement); in this case the composite image
really does replace two others, and their effects are combined
in an almost mathematical sense.

There is, then, a mechanistic level within the psychical
apparatus. We find a description of it at the beginning of the
Project for a Scientific Psychology, but it has to be pointed out
that Freud makes two mistakes. On the one hand, his mechanism, far from being modelled on latest insights of mechanics, as understood by physics, is simply outdated. His
other error, which is still more serious, is the attempt to
make it a primary mechanism governing the genesis of the
human being as such. We therefore have to situate this
'mechano-morphism' and restore it to its rightful place; its
position is certainly primal, but it does not lie at the origins
of human beings, or even at their psychological origins. It is
a corollary to a highly specific founding moment: the origin
of the drive and, to be more specific still, the origin of the so-
called sexual part-function, which has as its object the so-
called part-objects. It is not insignificant that it should be in
relation to the part-objects that Freud describes the notion of
the symbolic equation which makes it possible to slide from
one part-object to the next, as in the well-known equation
between child, faeces, phallus, breast, etc. In topographical
terms, this mechanomorphism can be situated at the deepest
level of the unconscious, in the darkest depths of its soul.
Finally, we also have to ask what it reproduces, what it
internalizes, bearing in mind, once again, that the process of
internalization does not preserve the internalized element
intact, but distorts it, often to such an extent that it becomes
unrecognizable.

Linguistico-Morphism

It is at this point that the question of the relationship between our last two 'morphisms' arises: could this level of the primary process, of freely mobile energy, which might be described as a mechano-morphism, also be described as 'linguistico-morphic', the reference being to a false linguistics? Is not the model a sort of 'language' which is never anchored and which never comes to an end, a 'language' in which signifiers circulate freely along innumerable paths of contiguity, similarity and contrast (cf. Laplanche, 1981; Laplanche and Leclaire, 1972)? Can we say that this is a false language, or a 'delinguified' language in the sense that we can speak of a false mechanics? Could it be that it is a very specific kind of mechanical language in that it operates in accordance with a Cartesian-style macro-mechanics? I first put forward this idea in the context of a critique of Lacan's famous adage to the effect that 'the unconscious is structured like a language', which I attempted to reformulate as 'the unconscious is a-non-structured like-a-language', a notion which obviously makes nonsense of the original. And that is what I mean when I speak of the mad mechanics or the mad linguistics of the primary process.

I therefore use the term 'morphisms' as an alternative way of referring this 'like a': like a body, like living substance, like a language; *this 'like a' is no longer like what it is*, if I can put it that way. And this in turn suggests the idea that there is a domain specific to psychoanalysis which is not 'like', or which is far from being like 'what it is'. Within this domain we find profoundly modified transpositions of neighbouring domains, but that does not mean that the psychoanalytic domain is constructed on the basis of − or emerges from − heterogeneous fields, or that it can in any sense be deduced from (or reduced to) a social-anthropology, a biology, a mechanics or a linguistics. My thesis as to the role of these neighbouring fields is that the domain specific to psycho-analysis emerges because it stands out against them, because it can be contrasted with them. But, I repeat, the fact that it

stands out means that the background does not remain
unchanged. Its emergence has a *foundational* import, just as
the gesture which creates the psychoanalytic situation has a
foundational import, a new foundational import.

2.6   Foundations and the historical-primal: psychoanalysis and psychology

The primal element in treatment necessarily relates to the historical-primal

These prologemena, which are also intended to have a
'cathartic' effect, are a gradual way of laying our foundations
for psychoanalysis. If we say that psychoanalysis cannot be
founded upon the disciplines from which it emerges, or
against which it stands out, do we imply that it can be
founded directly upon what it claims to be in the immediate,
or in other words upon its practice? Can we, without further
ado, derive from that practice a positive knowledge, a self-
reliant knowledge which borrows only from that practice? In
a sense, Freud's ambition is to do precisely that, or at least
that is one of the ways in which he *introduces* psychoanalysis.
But, as Freud himself also reminds us, there is, after all, a
difference between founding and introducing, which implies
starting with origins and constructing an object in the here
and now. At any rate, Freud is often forced to introduce
psychoanalysis by describing the analytic situation or the
immediate results of that situation, especially in his exposi-
tory works.

If we found psychoanalysis solely on what it takes to be its
fundamental situation and ignore all contingent factors, do we
not go back to what I described in connection with *the tub*,
namely a situation which founds itself, which creates its own
field and its own closure: the closure of the analytic session
and analytic treatment? But in the case of the tub, we have
to look at things more closely, as its closure is very relative.

It is not closed to everyday life in general; it is closed to
everyday life only in so far as it is the realm of interests. At
the same time its closure is tangential; in other words everything that occurs in everyday life is echoed inside it. What is
more important still, the analytic situation represents an
opening on to something else; it represents an interpretative
opening which can only be formulated in terms of unconscious wishes and, most important of all, in terms of a reference
to the *past*. The psychoanalytic tub is necessarily open to
the dimension of the *past*, and psychoanalytic interpretation
cannot forget that reference, even if it does constantly claim
that it stays in the *hic et nunc*. It is very fashionable to say
that we are dealing with a mythical past, or a 'mythical
child', but that is no more than word play. Of course we
mythologize the past, but we do so because we are looking
for a truth, because we are looking for more truth about the
past. We cannot simply tell patients in analysis, or anyone
who asks us about our knowledge, that we are creating
myths; what we have to explain is the fact that human
individuals create myths (and sometimes become victims of
myths), that they create myths about themselves. What is
this power to create myths, to theorize (and for the moment I
am using the terms interchangeably)? What does it work
upon, or in other words, what is this power to create myths,
to theorize (and for the moment I am using the terms interchangeably)? What does it work upon, or in other words,
what is there to be theorized in human beings? What are the
origins of this power and what are its first manifestations?
None of these questions can be left unanswered. In other
words, I am arguing that foundations for psychoanalysis
must be sought *in* a certain history, namely the history of
the appearance of the psychoanalytic subject, and that its
appearance must be situated *in relation to* the more general,
but non-psychoanalytic, history of the child.

Having adopted this general position, it is impossible to go
any further without examining the eminently complex relationship — and we are about to see why it has also been

distorted — between *psychoanalysis and psychology*, and especially *child psychology*. And this relationship must be examined at greater length than that between psychoanalysis and the 'related' sciences which I refer to generically as 'morphisms'.

At this point, we enter a minefield: the field of the 'genetic viewpoint'. It is a minefield of misunderstandings over words and things, where we find layer upon layer of quite unjustifiable but very tenacious retroactive effects. It is a domain where a kind of consensus has finally been reached on a number of theses which now seem to be beyond question, one being the thesis that psychoanalysis is a *general psychological theory* which is both unitary and capable of accounting for the entire development of the young human being and, ultimately, of human beings as such. Indeed, it is called upon to do so. Certain psychoanalysts take a cautious view of such claims, but others devote body and soul to the attempt to respond to the demand for a general psychology.

History, development, genesis and the primal

I said we were entering a minefield, and that is why I am unsure of whether I am going too fast or too slowly. The terms themelves are suspect: 'history', 'development', 'genesis', 'origin' . . ., we can take them or leave them, take them badly, or even take offence at them. Let us at least try to define the words we are going to be using, even though the definitions will always be somewhat approximate and will perhaps depend upon the mood of the moment. Whether we like it or not, *development* implies that something unfolds (*sich entwickelt* in German), that a potential that is already present unfolds, and that it does so in a predetermined order. Development implies a succession of phases and stages. 'Development' certainly deserves a better press than it usually gets: there is no reason to reject the notion, provided that it does not preclude mutations, reorganization and repetition; development does not necessarily imply continuity, and it can be dialectical. And nor does development necessarily imply that a simple, monadic unit develops its individual potential like a germ-cell or a seed. To be more accurate, subsets can be seen as the subject of development, or can be included in a unit: the most common type of subset to be found in descriptions of development is that which, when it comes the mother—child relationship, includes the mother or the environment in the initial unit. In other words, there is indeed a developmental viewpoint, and a legitimate psychology of development. Our real task is to restore it to its rightful place. There is *no* place for it in psychoanalysis, and restoring it to its rightful place therefore means that we have to locate psychoanalysis elsewhere, as no foundations for psychoanalysis can be be found in development. The appearance of the unconscious is an event which is not inscribed in any programme, even if we do include the mother's organism in the programme.

Genetic psychology?   It is difficult to see any great difference between these words and the words 'psychology of develop- ment', though the term 'genesis' does of course have much more far-reaching implications; the German for 'genesis' is *Entstehung* ('origin', or even 'creation').[13] As we do have to choose between these shifting meanings, I will take the option of making genetic psychology synonymous with 'psychology of development'. This is not the domain of the psychoanalyst in any real sense, but psychoanalysis does intervene within it. But this *inter-vention* must be understood in the strongest possible sense; psychoanalysis intervenes in the way that one interrupts a speaker to make an abrupt intervention; psychoanalysis intervenes in development, and the unconscious intervenes in the genetic. As I can refine my language only up to a certain point, I will not, however, ban the word 'genesis' in favour of the expression 'genesis of the unconscious', a term which refers, not to the develop- ment of the unconscious (a notion I have already rejected), but, on the contrary, to the emergence or appearance of the unconscious.

History   History too could involve us in a very lengthy debate, and I will do no more than allude to the issues involved. I do not reject the view that psychoanalysis must be founded upon a historical viewpoint, or in other words that it situates what it detects *in relation* to a temporal sequence. I am not of the opinion that, if we say that the unconscious appears, we must refuse to say at roughly what moment it does so, at least in the case of a determinate individual, or in what form we can detect its intervention, which implies, by definition, that we have to state that it was not present until a given moment. I will not refer to any great extent to what has been called 'the new history'. This modern school has made a number of productive innovations and one of its most progressive features is, it would seem, its hostility to event-bound history [*l'événementiel*]. It is claimed that event-bound history has been banished from the scene, but I tend to take the view that the event has been put in its rightful place, that it has been situated in relation to its conditions of possibility and of emergence; this is one of the primary meanings of the history of mentalities or even archaeology (in Foucault's sense). In so far as it too adopts a historical viewpoint (to a certain extent), psychoanalysis must also adopt two interrelated theses: the *événementiel*, trauma and childhood events are still essential points of reference; but when we examine more universal situations, we also hope to bring out something resembling, *mutatis mutandis*, an 'archaeology'; not only the framework in which one or another event is inscribed, not only the background against which events stand out, but also that which allows an event to exist, that which gives it its psychoanalytic specificity.

To use the term 'structure' to describe the non-event-bound foundations of the event would imply a very loose use of a term which, regrettable as it may be, has been irremediably marked by structuralist dogma (Laplanche, 1979a). I still prefer to use the old Freudian term 'primal', even if I do use it in a rather personal sense. The term is used to translate the prefix *ur-* and the adjective *ursprünglich*. The primal is something which transcends time but which is also bound up with time. I will develop the idea of a primal situation which can, in my view, explain the intervention and emergence of the unconscious, the drive and the apparatus of the soul.

I have defined the meaning of a few words, but that is not enough to clear up all the misunderstandings, particularly where origins are concerned. I refer to the accretion of countless meanings, to the back-projection of the adult on to the child, and to the cumulative assertions that have been repeated so often that they have become more opaque, more impenetrable and more stubborn than the facts themselves (I am thinking here of certain 'psychoanalytic' theses). Take the theses about the objectless state, about primary narcissism, or Klein's theses. Freud himself is not above using a slippery terminology and indulging in paralogisms; he too can confuse fields and make them overlap. The confusion over points of view destroys many an important insight. But if we then look at the post-Freudian heritage, all the guidelines disappear, as does what I call Freud's call to order. And that is rather more serious.

Given that it is quite complex, allow me to explain my initial position once more. I am arguing that in looking for foundations for psychoanalysis, we cannot avoid referring to history; that its foundations must, in that sense, be historical or genetic; but I am using those terms to refer to the genesis of the primal, and not in the narrow sense in which genetic psychology understands them. In other words, the foundations of psychoanalysis are not up in the air; I reject as facile the idea of 'myths' and references to so-called 'mythical times', regardless of whether they refer to individual history or collective history. But at the same time, we have to delineate the foundations of psychoanalysis, as opposed to developmental psychology, and that can only be done by stressing the specificity of its object: the unconscious and sexuality.

The vicariousness of sexuality and self-preservation ...

Why is it that it is so difficult to differentiate between the genesis of the primal and the genetics of the developmental? It is because human beings *spontaneously reinvest* or *recathect*, if I can put it that way, the whole of psychical life with sexual motivations which are to a great extent unconscious. Sexuality, I repeat, vicariously supports the human instinct for self-preservation, and that instinct is to some extent lacking. I propose to illustrate my point with the following image: think of a large building constructed over a period of hundreds, or even thousands, of years, such as a palace or a protohistoric temple which has been rebuilt or extended in the course of its evolution (see figure 2.1). Each sovereign, or each generation of priests, adds a stratum to the new building, but the point is that techniques and materials have changed in the intervening years (otherwise my illustration will not work). Sun-dried mud bricks have given way to stone, drystone walls to masonry.

If we build in stone on foundations of mud brick, the foundations will obviously collapse. Do we have to rebuild

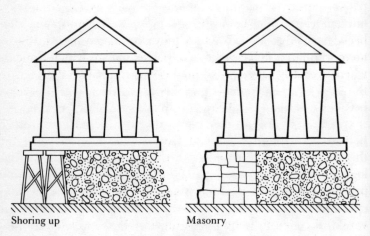

Shoring up   Masonry

Figure 2.1

everything, or is it possible to shore the temple up? Shoring it up simply means supporting the building, excavating the foundations and recementing them in order to strengthen them — the current technique involves 'injecting' concrete. I am obviously using this image to illustrate how sexuality supports self-preservation in human beings. Shoring up, however, is obviously not the same thing as vicariance, as all the work is done at once, whereas the establishment of a vicarious relationship is a gradual, piecemeal process: the sexual development of a child does not suddenly underpin or support its psychological development once and for all. What is more, vicariousness is not simply a temporal process; unconscious sexual motivations are constantly, ceaselessly, being fed or injected into a flagging instinct for self-preservation and giving it a new coherence.

... *Is the real foundation for the pansexual and panpsychoanalytic illusion*

There is, then, in human beings, a natural, or at least spontaneous, tendency to shore up self-preservation with sexuality; and that tendency is another name for what I call pansexualism. Pansexualism was a state and tendency of human reality long before it became the aberration that has been ascribed to Freud. As for panpsychoanalyticism, that is no more than a debased form of pansexualism which appears when sexuality is, because of this vicariousness, debased to the level of an 'object-relation', or when the strict distinction between the sexual and the non-sexual ceases to be observed.

It is then by way of this *highly specific* vicarious relationship between the non-sexual and the sexual in human beings that I intend to approach, and then criticise, the epistemologically vicarious relationship between psychoanalysis and psychology. Whilst I am attempting to denounce certain epistemological errors which lead to fields being confused, I would also like to issue a solemn warning: it must never be forgotten that these errors occur because the human subject itself leads us astray because it (like our architect) it has altered the foundations of its building.

In the rather different context of a discussion of hysterics and of the seduction theory (and it would not be difficult to show that the two are not unrelated), Freud (1950, pp. 352—9) uses the expression *proton pseudos*, meaning of course 'first lie', but also 'first error' or, so to speak, 'first objective lie', or 'first fallacy' *[premier fallace]*, as I sometimes translate it. A hysteric is not someone who lies for the sake of lying; there is a lie within the hysterogenic situation itself. I propose that we extend or shift the meaning of the term, and say that there is a *proton pseudos* at work in human beings, that it founds the psychoanalytic domain, and that it has constant epistemological repercussions which we perceive as a host of errors. In order to correct these errors, we have to grasp their mechanisms. Simply returning to Freud is out of the question; as will be demonstrated below, he too succumbs to this fallacy. What I am trying to demonstrate is that all these errors are 'well founded', that they are based upon a very real human propensity: the movement of knowledge tends to complete a movement in the real, to bring it *to a climax*.

Psychoanalysis and psychology: A faulty joint

A multitude of illusions may arise here, but they can easily be summed up: the basic illusion is that psychoanalysis can be incorporated into a general psychology. To say that psychoanalysis believes that it has something to say about everything, that is thinks it can *intervene* (to readopt the expression we used earlier) in everything, means using those claims as a pretext for saying that it *is* everything, and for *actively promoting* its claims to being a universal form of knowledge.

In order to deflate the pretensions of psychoanalysis, we may have to digress somewhat. First of all, it has to be shown that the situation is not quite the same when we are

talking about adults and about children, and when we are
talking about relations between adults and children (and
those relations are both epistemological and real). A
number of dubious ways of approaching this issue have been
proposed; they are in fact complementary.

The psychoanalytic psychology of the adult

The first of these consists in the attempt to extend findings
obtained with the psychoanalytic method into a general
adult psychology. This is a universal tendency within the
Freudian movement: the apparatus of the soul is described as
a generalized psychical apparatus, and a general explanation
of human actions and behaviour is put forward on the basis
of that apparatus and especially of its so-called 'ego' or
'consciousness-perception' aspects. Here we have the most
official part of the Freudian heritage, namely the American
school (Hartmann) which achieved a maximal level of psy-
chologization when it encountered Rapaport, a psychologist
who was only too happy to have at last found a suitable
doctrine for his purposes. But many other schools produce
similar results, even though they may look very different; the
Kleinians are certainly convinced that psychoanalysis is the
only psychology, the most formalized, but also the most
generalized claim to that effect being, of course, that made
by Bion. I say that this is an illusion but, when we are
dealing with adults, it may be a well-founded illusion as,
in the case of adults, we are unable to delineate a psychological field which is not constantly being recathected and
reinvested by unconscious sexual motivations. It is therefore
no accident that non-psychoanalytic adult psychology
should have withered away. It remains to be seen whether
psychoanalysis itself might not have withered away in the
course of this process of withering away and extension;
whether it might not have lost sight of the specificity of its
own approach, its specificity being that it is confined to what

I depict as a tub which derives from a tangential field of
'interests' without ever merging with it.

Whilst there are few, if any, forms of adult psychology
which do not claim to take their inspiration from psychoanalysis to some extent, we have yet to demonstrate that
there is no possibility of a non-psychoanalytic psychology
being *articulated* with psychoanalysis. To take the example of
The Interpretation of Dreams once more, one cannot fail to
be struck by its ambitions: it seeks to elaborate a general
psychology of dreams which goes far beyond the specifically
psychoanalytic problem of their interpretation. It is no
coincidence that the last chapter should be entitled 'The
Psychology of the Dream Processes'. A new and innovative
reading reveals the extent to which truly psychological
problems are left unresolved; they have to be completely
reworked, starting with a more accurate phenomenological
description of precisely what is meant by a 'dream within a
dream'. [14]

Reinjecting psychoanalytic concepts into child psychology

Whilst there may be some excuse for panpsychoanalyticism
when we are dealing with adults, given that adults are completely recathected by the sexual, a similar approach to child
psychology is more fundamentally flawed, regardless of
whether the findings of adult psychoanalysis are back-
projected on to children or whether those elements within the
specific domain of childhood which pertain to psychoanalysis
are confused with elements accessible to psychology or
psycho-sociology. The confusion takes different forms. On
the one hand, concepts derived from the psychoanalytic
situation can be back-projected — and here I am obviously
referring to Melanie Klein; on the other, use can be made
of bastardized concepts such as 'symbiosis' or 'interaction'.
Basically, there is little difference between these two approaches. The concepts that are derived from analysis, from
the psychoanalytic situation, from psychoanalytic observ-

ation, or even from non-clinical psychoanalysis, may come from work with adults (as do the concepts of narcissism and auto-eroticism, or stages of sexual development) or from work with both children and adults (Melanie Klein's 'positions' are a case in point; they derive from analytic situations involving either adults or children), but there is always an element of retroprojection or retrointrojection. The theoretical and practical issues raised by these alternative approaches may of course seem to be different: that depends on whether the concepts which are mistakenly reintrojected into childhood do or do not retain their psychoanalytic rigour. If the concepts do retain their rigour (but can they?), we have a false psychoanalytic child psychology, though it does often have to be given credit for flaunting its falsity by raising the banner of *myth* or *the mythical child*. This tendency is represented by the nineteenth volume of the *Nouvelle Revue de Psychanalyse* (1979, L'Enfant), which is now somewhat dated but still very instructive. Alternatively, the concepts that are reinjected may be debased so as to lend more credence to the image of development they generate. Both tendencies are equally dangerous in that they indicate a complete failure to grasp the psychoanalysis − psychology articulation. We are always offered a mixture of psychoanalysis and psychology. In other words, there is always a discrepancy between the psychoanalytic child and the child under observation; at the same time, psychoanalytic concepts have to be debased if they are to apply to the actual infant who is under observation. It is simply not the case that one alternative is preferable to the other; they make each other worse.

Where children are concerned, there is, then, a basic scientific illusion, and it is bound up with the *proton pseudos*. It cannot be stressed too often that the psychoanalytic discovery is the discovery of the unconscious and of sexuality, in the sense in which Freud defines those terms. Within the psychoanalytic situation, it is possible to describe certain states, stages and a certain genesis, and they relate specifi-

cally to the psychoanalytic domain itself (whether the discussion centres on adults or children is irrelevant; Melanie
Klein demonstrates more than adequately that children
can participate in the analytic situation). This is why
psychoanalysts, or at least a good number of them, are under
the illusion that they can detect situations which are not
stages in infantile sexuality (and it is far from easy to detect
even those stages) but stages in the evolution of the broader
relationship between the child and its world. We are wit-
nessing the effects of pansexualism once more. But whenever
pansexualism begins to rear its head, and whenever sexuality
claims to be everything (or, as in the present case, to claim
that the stages of infantile sexuality are the sum total of the
individual's relationship with his environment), sexuality
becomes meaningless. If psychoanalysis can say everything
there is to be said about child psychology, sexuality disappears altogether, as we can see from the various attempts
that have been made to construct a pansexualism and
especially from Jung's attempt to do so.

Psychologists intoxicated by panpsychoanalyticism

Curiously enough, the psychologists themselves are deluded
by these reinjections; one has only to open a book of child
psychology at random to see how what is conventionally, and
as it happens without pejorative intent, referred to as the
psychoanalytically inspired model is granted the same
credence as the theses of Piaget or any other exponent of
direct psychological observation. The model can then be
made to accommodate points of view as divergent as those of
Spitz, Mahler, Winnicott and Melanie Kelin, not to mention
Freud, though he in fact tends to be somewhat forgotten.
The credence which is granted without any justification
whatsoever to so-called analytic theories of development, is
simply an indirect tribute to the persuasively intoxicating
powers of panpsychoanalyticism, and the secret behind its

dynamism is to be found in the spontaneous pansexualism of human beings.[15]

Conceptual reductionism

The situation is, then, one of total confusion. With the exception of those who take refuge in 'myths', the psycho-analysts find themselves in agreement with the psychologists, and the psychologists are prepared to make some use of notions and sequences derived from the psychoanalytic view

Table 2.1

Object of sexual *Wunsch* (wish)	Object of need and perception perception guides life perception guides need

(whereas Freud, as we shall see, derives one from the other)

Objectality: refinding a sexual object by following path traced by *Wunsch*	Objectivity: delineation and positioning of independent motor-perceptive object as independent (Piaget, etc.)
Hallucinatory wish fulfilment (with dream as model)	Insertion of a supposedly hallucinatory stage into access to external reality.
Sexual narcissism	Absence of real object non-differentiation between subject and object, symbioisis, etc.

of the development of human sexuality, as though their discussions of the stages of the constitution of the object or of the stages of the understanding of logical relations dealt with the same topic as a psychoanalytic discussion of stages. The consensus of opinion between psychoanalytic child psychologists and those who take a more experimental view provides the basis for the terminological reductionism shown in the two columns of table 2.1.

This reductionism results in more than conceptual confusion; phases and stages of development are being superimposed. The whole of development is being described in terms which Freud applies specifically to the emergence of sexuality. But just as Freudian pychoanalysis gains a hold on development, it is emptied of its substance because the whole evolution of the child is desexualized.

2.7   A major instance of confusion: The 'objectless' state

Splitting Freud on narcissism

To take a prime example: the gross confusion brought about by the notions of narcissism and primary narcissism. Here, we have to split Freud himself. Why do we assume that we have the right to do so, or the right to choose 'our' Freud, the 'good' Freud as opposed to the 'bad'? To do so would be quite unacceptable *unless we can demonstrate the existence of the reductionism, and explain its mechanisms*. Our only option is to undo the confusion we have discussed at such length.

The other thing which makes it legitimate to 'split' Freud in this way is the presence, within the basic texts, of erratic warning passages which *call us to order* or tell us to *get a grip on ourselves*, which warn us that psychoanalysis is something other than what Freud has just been describing, that it may involve a reversal of perspective. Thus, at the very moment when he uses the phrase 'primary narcissism of children' –

an expression which is at best ambiguous and at worst potentially disastrous — Freud clearly gives us to understand that the only narcissism that affects 'His Majesty the Baby' (1914, p. 91) is the narcissism of the parents who project on to the child their own self-love and, of course, the wishful dreams they never carried out. It is therefore essential to undertake an interpretative reading, and that involves splitting; we have to work through Freud's texts, but we do not necessarily have to take them in chronological order. There is no such thing as a pure proto-Freud and then an absent-minded deutero-Freud, particularly where the question of narcissism is concerned. I will therefore not enter into a detailed discussion of this reductionism, and will simply refer the reader to the relevant articles on auto-erotism, narcissism, and primary and secondary narcissism in *The Language of Psychoanalysis* (Laplanche and Pontalis, 1973) and to Vichyn's more acerbic article on the birth of the concepts of auto-crotism and narcissism (Vichyn, 1984).

The successive moments of the erotic

What do we find in Freud? A line that can be traced, and which later becomes more complex: autoerotism — narcissism — object-choice. This is a chronological line, a line of descent; there can be no avoiding the issue by claiming that we are dealing with a false time or a mythical genesis: the three positions do come one after the other. It is immediately obvious that the line does not start with narcissism; and narcissism is, so to speak, in good company, with the erotic to the left of it and the erotic to the right of it: first we have auto-erotism, and then object-choice, and we know that, for Freud, that can only mean the choice of a love-object. It will obviously be objected that the change in terminology has to be explained; first we have auto-*erotism*, and then we have *love* ... but the whole point is that it is narcissism which is called upon to provide the explanation.

Auto-erotism is not primary

Let us first recall the four characteristics of auto-erotism or of the auto-erotic 'stage', given that we do have to use the term. It refers primarily to an immediate satisfaction obtained in one or another part of the body, at the very spot where the excitation occurs: this is what Freud calls organ pleasure. It is a non-unified, fragmented satisfaction which has nothing to do with other organs or, *a fortiori*, the body as a whole, and which is exhausted at the point where it is born; a polypary of pleasures would be an appropriate image. On the other hand, as the 'auto'- prefix indicates, auto-erotism has *no external object*; neither a person nor even a part-object. Finally, auto-erotic activity cannot be defined without reference to *fantasy*, or to the fantasy object, which is not quite the same thing. Witness the fact that any psycho-analyst confronted with an analysand whose behaviour is 'auto-erotic' immediately looks for and uncovers the under-lying fantasy: no one masturbates without having fantasies, and the thing about masturbation that interests the analyst is the fantasy. This is not true of adults alone: the dimension of a fantasy representation, and therefore the dimension of memory, is assumed from the outset. It is assumed to exist even at the level of the oral prototype of auto-erotism: 'Furthermore, it is clear that the behaviour of a child who indulges in thumb-sucking is determined by a search for some pleasure which has already been experienced and is now remembered' (Freud, 1905, p. 181).

I stressed earlier that narcissism is part of a sequence. The inescapable conclusion to be drawn from that is that it comes second and not first: auto-erotism − narcissism − object-choice. But does this necessarily mean that auto-erotism is the very first term in the sequence or the very first stage in the concrete development of the individual? In a celebrated passage (1905, p. 46), Freud asserts that this is not the case:

At a time at which the first beginnings of sexual satisfaction are still linked with the taking of nourishment, the sexual drive has a sexual object outside the infant's own body in the shape of its mother's breast. It is only later that the instinct loses that object ... The sexual drive *then becomes auto-erotic,* and not until the period of latency has been passed is the original relation restored ... The finding of an object is in fact a refinding of it. [My italics.]

I have discussed this passage at length elsewhere (Laplanche, 1976), and it is of crucial importance to the theory of leaning on, but, as I shall explain, I am now trying to get beyond that theory. For our present purposes, it should be noted that auto-erotism does not come first in any absolute sense, even though it is the first independent stage of sexuality; it does not represent the beginning of the child's relations with the world, but it is characteristic of what we might call the 'auto' period, and that implies turning away from the world.

Narcissism: a sexual moment of unification

Let us now move on from auto-erotism to narcissism. How can we characterize narcissism in relation to this initial turning away from the world? In Freud's most explicit texts, it is defined in terms of the concentration of auto-erotism (which is essentially dispersed) on to a single object. But that object itself is also an 'auto' object; it is always an internal, 'reflected' object, and that is why it is named after the hero of the mirror: Narcissus. That reflected object is caught up in a play of interlocking images: the body, a certain unified image of the body, or the 'ego'. Freud's cardinal and in-augural text (1914, pp. 76–7) reads as follows, but all too often it is ignored, and its radical nature is overlooked:

What is the relation of the narcissism of which we are now speaking to auto-erotism, which we have described as an early state of the libido? [The distinction is clear: an early state of the libido is not synonymous with an early state of the individual.] ... we are bound to suppose that a unity comparable to the ego canot exist in the individual from the start; the ego has to be developed. The auto-erotic drives, however, are there from the very first; so there must be something added to auto-erotism — a new psychical action — in order to bring about narcissism [two comments are called for here: according to Freud, this is an explicitly temporal sequence, and not a mythical sequence; the birth of narcissism is absolutely correlative to the birth of the ego].

This sequence (auto-erotism, narcissism, object-choice), which we are trying to reduce to its bare essentials, has nothing to do with the individual; it concerns the individual's sexual life, sexual drive and sexual object. And that sexual life stands out against the backdrop of a pre-existing non-sexual life or relationship, of a life dominated by needs; it will be separated out from that life.

Chronology of auto-erotism and narcissism

The notions of leaning on and of an 'auto' period mean that sexual life is not something that exists from the very first. To put it more clearly, its beginnings should not be confused with the beginnings of relational life. They also mean that (for Freud at least) this is the only primary or primal narcissism; no auto-erotism can be more primal than this. I therefore conceptualize sexual life as something which is, so to speak, grafted on to or which emerges from (I leave that question open) a relational life (which in the period 1910−15 is characterized in terms of self-preservative instincts, or in terms of need). Here, an important question arises: the question of steps or stages. How are we to conceptualize the sequence of 'auto-erotism, narcissism, homosexuality (which Freud briefly intercalates into the sequence) heterosexual object-choice'? How are we to articulate it with, or make it correspond to, the many other sequences and chronological tables of which psychoanalysts are so fond: the sequence of oral, anal and genital stages, all the stages Ferenczi (1926) describes in connection with the development of a 'sense of reality', not to mention Klein's sequence of positions, or the

'autism, symbiosis, separation, individuation' sequence?
How does it correspond to the gradual and maturational
evolution of the subject's relationship with the objective
world (which can now be described in more refined terms
than those used by Piaget)? Is there such a thing as a series
of sexual stages which we can locate in a purely temporal
chronology? If we say that the auto-erotism, narcissism,
object-choice sequence is grafted on to relational life, do we
therefore have to say that it begins at, say, the age of two
months, or six months? Certainly not. Once we get away
from the idea that Freud's stages are stages in the life of
the individual there is no justification for the unthinking
introduction of a new set of stages.

The terms auto-erotism and narcissism do not define basic
modes of relating to the world in general, but modes of
sexual functioning and modes of pleasure. Those modes are
separated out from a broader relationship with the world,
which continues to evolve and progress, and they must
therefore be conceived as *moments* which are, to a greater
or lesser extent, both *punctual* and *reiterated*, the essential
difference between the two being a matter of their temporal
status. A two-stage sequence — sexual satisfaction bound up
with need, and then a retreat into auto-erotism — is repeated
on innumerable occasions. But there is absolutely no reason
to suppose that these micro-sequences mechanically combine
to produce a third stage which completes the triad of leaning
on, auto-erotism and narcissism. Given that it is essentially
a matter of unification, or even of solidification, primary narcissism is more likely to lend itself to an evolution which
takes the form of structuring moments, and it is important
that one of the most important stages in its emergence should
have been described by Lacan (1949) as the moment of a
mutation: the mirror stage. Not that the mirror stage is the
alpha and omega of narcissism, but it is prototypical of
the crucial moments of precipitation, solidification or
crystalization (and it is no coincidence that the latter term
should also be used in connection with love). Once we begin

to locate narcissism within a sexual sequence, it is, however, absurd to speak of a pure narcissistic phase. Freud himself points that out in connection with the third of our stages (object-choice): at this stage, the choice of narcissistic object and the choice of an object by leaning on coexist and are constantly interwoven.

Object-choice and access to objectivity: the Freudian roots of the confusion

'Object-choice' means, of course, choice of sexual object. How is it that, in psychoanalytic thought, this type of sequence can be collapsed into a sequence punctuating access to *objectivity*? How could Freud himself conflate the two? The confusion has a long history. It is not as though there was once a time when everything was perfectly clear, and then a moment when everything became confused. The confusion occurred before the theory was formulated. The theory did not evolve in linear fashion towards the reductionism that I am denouncing. It has to be stated that the reduction of sexuality to self-preservation came about even before the theory of narcissism was formulated with any clarity. Concrete evidence of that can be found in three texts: 'On Narcissism: an Introduction' (Freud, 1914), 'Formulations on the Two Principles of Mental Functioning' (Freud, 1911a) and 'Instincts and their Vicissitudes' (Freud 1915a). I hold something of a grudge against the 'Formulations' (perhaps that is why I translated it) precisely because that is the text which founds the psychoanalytic child psychology, which I regard as the source of all the confusion.

Reduction of sexual evolution to self-preservation

The opening pages of the 'Formulations' give an explicit description of the evolution of the ego or self-preservative drives. It is only in the third section that the sexual drives are mentioned, but Freud immediately adds that things are not quite the same where they are concerned. Fine, so far, so good. Has the distinction been established? No. On the contrary: throughout the first four pages, the development of the self-preservative drives is described in terms of a sequence modelled on the sexual sequence, beginning with a primal, closed state (whereas in the sexual domain, the 'auto' stage was the result of a process and not an absolute origin). It then requires all sorts of contortions — the contortions typical of all idealism — to get out of that state; how can a self-enclosed idealism open out on to the world? All idealisms get themselves into contortions in their attempts to recover what they have lost. What I am denouncing as idealism, or as a biological solipsism, reaches its apotheosis in the opening pages of Freud's 'Formulations'. The self-preservative drives, the psycho-biological individual and the infant all have to learn the way to the object, and a whole series of successive psychical functions then has to be introduced by making deductions based upon a highly improbable rational psychology: consciousness, attention, memory, judgement, and so on. Indeed, the text could be recruited to the 'symbiosis' cause, if we also take into account the famous note (pp. 219—20n.) which makes the care the infant receives from its mother (*not* the mother herself) part of the initial 'egg'. Even before there has been any real 'introduction' to narcissism (Freud, 1914) its fate has been prefigured or even sealed.

Reduction of self-preservative functioning to sexual drive

The other exemplary text is 'Instincts and their Vicissitudes' (Freud, 1915a), where a symmetrical reduction is effected: here, it is self-preservation that is reduced to sexuality, and not sexuality that is reduced to self-preservation. It is explicitly stated that the initial model is sexuality; self-preservation is largely overlooked, as the text deals with the vicissitudes of the sexual drives. But despite this promising start it is, as I have argued elsewhere (Laplanche, 1980c, p.

38ff.), necessary to slip a knife into the cracks; I have also
shown how we have to split Freud's description of the drives.
Without wishing to go over the same arguments again,
let me point out one vital but ambiguous formula (Freud,
1915a, p. 134n.) as it is a veritable compromise formation:
'The ego-drives, which are never capable of auto-erotic
satisfaction...'. Wonderful! The bio-psychological individual, with his self-preservative drives (or 'ego drives') is,
from the outset, open to object-intentionality., There is also
an amazing degree of confusion at the terminological level: is
it a truism to say that the self-preservative drives, which are
by definition non-erotic, are not capable of auto-erotic
satisfaction, or is it nonsense? It is more likely to be simply
inaccurate; the meaning of auto-erotism is distorted, and is
in danger of losing its sexual connotations, of implying that
the subject is self-contained, that it has no external object,
sexual or non-sexual. We have here a further instance of the
reductionism we are trying to undo.

Freud supports objectlessness

To end this schematic account of Freud's reductionism, it
will be recalled that, in subsequent texts, primary or primal
narcissism will be assumed to be the earliest stage of the
human being, and will no longer be differentiated from
autoerotism. In Freud's later writings, the auto-erotism—
narcissism sequence disappears; auto-erotism is defined as
the mode of satisfaction appropriate to the narcissistic stage.
Primary narcissism is therefore no longer defined in terms of
a characteristically specular relation with an internal object,
and in effect becomes synonymous with 'objectless state'. As
the cards are reshuffled, the 'narcissism of the ego' also
acquires a new role: in 'On Narcissism: An Introduction', it
is an equivalent to primary narcissism, as there has to be
some initial action on the part of the ego if narcissism is to
exist. No ego means no narcissism. But in later texts, and
especially in *The Ego and the Id* (Freud, 1923, p. 46), the

narcissism of the ego, as opposed to objectless primary narcissism, is said to be secondary.

The confusion I am denouncing, or the reduction of the genesis of sexuality to the development of perceptivo-motor relations with the world or the environment, continues to wreak havoc long after Freud. If the subject, drives included, so to speak, is initially a closed system, how can it then become open? There is talk of 'frustration', and of how it teaches the little human being to live, but the whole point is that Freud's *Versagnung* does not mean frustration — or not simply frustration. It is an act of refusal on the part of another adult human being, a 'refusal to' or, as I would now translate it, *'un refusement'* ['a refusing'].

Confusion over 'primary hallucinations'

The notion of primary hallucination, and the confusion to which it has given rise, is something else that has to be called into question, even though it has been used so often since Freud's day that it has come to be seen as an established fact. We know that the notion originates from the *Project for a Scientific Psychology*, where Freud refers (1950, p. 318) to what he calls the 'experience of satisfaction', which presupposes, of course, that the subject has some primary awareness of the world and can therefore obtain satisfaction. And then (p. 319) we are told that, in the absence of satisfaction, the object will be hallucinated. If the child can find food in hallucinatory fashion, why should it emerge from this state? Why should a little frustration be tolerable thanks to hallucination, and why should a lot of frustration make it renounce hallucinations? What Freud is describing here is in a sense the appearance or genesis of sexuality. We find here another instance of reductionism, especially in the work of Freud's heirs. In the *Project* it is the *indications that accompany satisfaction* that are hallucinated, and not the object of satisfaction. In the prototypical example, the almost fictive model of suckling, breast and milk do not coincide; there is a displacement from breast to milk. The 'hallucination' does not substitute an imaginary real for the real, or one form of food for another. The same point can be made with respect to another example, which seems to take the notion of substitute satisfaction further still: the hunger dreams studied by Freud in *The Interpretation of Dreams* A so-called primary hallucination feeds no one; the hallucination is not a substitute for reality; it represents the birth of fantasy, a destroyed from the sexual line. No primary hallucination (if there is such a thing) has ever been destroyed by reality. And no hallucination can be destroyed in that way. (We will come back to this schema which, as it stands, is not yet satisfactory; it belongs to the so-called leaning construct, a construct which is no more than a moment in a transition towards something else. Leaning on, as such, still implies an apparently endogenous process of development; the human being is certainly present from the start in the 'experience of satisfaction — learning on' schema, but its only role is to absent itself.

Symbiosis

We have already mentioned another avatar of this reductionism: the inclusion of the mother in the initial 'egg'. This opens up the way for what has been termed a dyad, a dualism or even symbiosis. The latter term leads to all sorts of confusion, despite its apparent simplicity. Symbiosis is a biological notion, and perhaps an objective notion, but attempts have been made to use it to promote the idea of a subjective symbiosis. In biological terms it refers, according to the *Robert* dictionary, to 'a lasting and mutually profitable association between two living organisms'; the example given refers to lichen. But even in biological terms, even in terms of self-preservation, there is something dubious about the notion that the mother—child association is profitable for both parties. It also involves profound dissymmetries. To take a different biological model of association, we could equally well say that the child is a parasite which lives off its mother. Conversely, we might, to play on the French meaning of *parasite* [interference, atmospherics], say that the mother prevents her child from communicating.

Two ill-founded reactions to the solipsism of the psychoanalytic baby

I have attempted to show that all these theoretical tendencies to reduce sexuality to self-preservation stem from a real vicarious relationship, from the way in which sexuality under-pins self-preservation, and that is most definitely a complex process which has to be seen as being gradual and fragmentary. If we transpose this process into one in which love takes complete charge of the interests of self-preservation by love, and if we further postulate that it has done so throughout all eternity, we are flying in the face of the facts and setting ourselves an impossible task (compounded by a caricaturally solipsist philosophy): getting the subject out of its monad, and pulling the world out of the conjuror's hat.

Balint

One of the most violent reactions against the theory of primary narcissism is to be found in Balint's 'Early Developmental States of the Ego. Primary Object-Love' (Balint,1937). In the theoretical section of his article, he completely dismisses the notion of objectless primary narcissism. But he remains within the general trend in that he replaces primary narcissism with the term 'Primary object-love', and thereby makes the sexual hegemonic from the outset. Love, or the erotic? In any event, the introduction of the term 'love' at this early stage creates more problems than it solves, in that all psychoanalytic investigations show that love is not simply a relationship based upon an attachment to the other; it means taking the other into consideration as a totality. It is an act on the part of a total subject. As Freud (1915a, p.137) puts it, 'we are not in the habit of saying of a single sexual drive that it loves its object'. By back-projecting love on to the earliest subject-environment relationship, Balint tends to make us overlook the fact that Eros has its own separate genesis, and that narcissistic totalization is a major stage within that genesis. I say all this to indicate that, whilst I welcome the clarity of Balint's critique, I have my doubts about the introduction of the term 'primary love', which takes us back to the very reductionism that I am trying to exorcise.

The Kleinians

And what of the Kleinians? The Kleinians infiltrate Freud's thought until such time as they can detonate an explosion from within. They gradually inject their project into Freud's terminology with such a degree of success that the term primary narcissism continues to be used. What they are describing in this context is a kind of object-relation, which makes a happy contrast with the notion of absolute narcissism. The Kleinian concept of narcissism first sees the light of day in *Developments in Psychoanalysis* (Klein et al.,1952), together with a critique, sometimes implicit, sometimes explicit, of the notion of monadic closure. The following formulation is taken from Paula Heimann's contribution (Heimann,1952, pp. 153–4): 'In the narcissistic condition the external object is hated and rejected, so that one loves the internal object which is fused with the self and experience pleasure from it.' The narcissistic condition implies the cathecting of an object, of something internal which fuses with the ego. What is more, that narcissistic condition is perfectly compatible with an early awareness of the world and the external object, if only in terms of hate and rejection. As Kleinian thought develops, narcissism appears to become more and more closely bound up with an internalized internal object. As Joan Riviere puts it in her general introdution to the volume (Riviere,1952, p. 13): 'In our view the narcissistic or auto-erotic phase overlaps and co-exists with object-relation, largely owing to the important introjective processes operating at this stage.' Melanie Klein uses similar arguments against the monadic state in her 'On Observing the Behaviour of Young Infants' (1952a). To conclude, the Kleinians begin to outline a theory which gets away from the fable that human beings originally live in a narcissistic state, and to elaborate the only tenable concept of narcissism: it is bound up with the introjection of a whole object.[16]But, rather as in the case of Balint, the threat of reductionism is still present because the entire process of development is explicitly subsumed under the love—hate dyad alone, and because not a word is said about self-preservation.

2.8 A role for child psychology

One of the major obstacles that prevents us from arriving at a sound view of the specificity of psychoanalysis, and of the relationship between the psychoanalytic field, the psychological field and the early development of the human being is the failure to make a distinction between the domain of sexuality and that of early psycho-physiological adaptation, or what Freud himself termed self-preservation before he too abandoned that notion.

The psychoanalytic child: a 'mythical child'? Discussion of André Green

Given the aporia bequeathed us by Freud, and the way in which he himself introduces a degree of theoretical confusion, the most radical reaction is, of course, to divorce the psychoanalytic line from all psychology, as, in their various ways, do Balint and the Kleinians, or even to fall back upon the 'mythical child' or the 'psychoanalytic child'. This is the theme of a number of the articles which appeared in the nineteenth volume of the *Nouvelle Revue de Psychanalyse* (Spring, 1979), which was devoted to 'the child'. André Green's article on 'The model child' (Green,1979, p. 45) argues along

these lines, and falls back upon the notion of 'the psychoanalytic child', meaning the child as defined both by the analytic
situation and by analytic theory:

> This necessarily involves us in a discussion the terms of
> which were defined by Anna Freud: is the 'real' child the
> child that is constructed, or reconstructed, by psychoanalysis?
> My answer is an unequivocal 'No'. But I would also add that
> it is not the role of psychoanalysis to reconstruct the real
> child. The mythical child, or the mythical childhood of the
> real child is, rather, the object of child psychology [we are
> about to witness the introduction of an opposition between
> myth and psychoanalysis, and reality and psychology]. I
> would therefore make a distinction between the true child of
> psychoanalysis — 'true' in the sense in which Freud speaks of
> historical truth — and the real child of psychology. At the
> higher level of the material truth, the child can only be a
> combination of the real child of psychology and the true child
> of psychoanalysis.

Green's suggestion has to be described as sound or salutary
in that he quite rightly locates the field of psychoanalysis by
distinguishing it from another field: that of psychology. But,
in my view, Green fails to locate the distinction correctly.
The only way in which he can locate it is by brutally reducing
psychology to the level of a pseudo-science which deals solely
with the 'real', by denying it the right to use hypotheses and
to appeal to, for example, the hypothesis of the psychical
representative, which is, according to Green, a central notion
in psychoanalysis. Even assuming that we do go along with
certain of his arguments, a whole series of questions arises.
First of all, the concept of a mythical or representative child,
does not, it seems to me, get to the bottom of the matter. In
order to do that, we have both to recognize that the human
subject, or the child, has a remarkable talent for creating its
own myths, and to maintain the distinction between self-
representations and scientific hypotheses. In more general

terms, Green appears to me to alternate between using two different criteria in his attempt to delineate a domain specific to psychoanalysis. Sometimes he uses the *unconscious* as a criterion, and there I am in full agreement with him (even though I insist that we have to characterize it as being sexual through and through). At other times he claims that the specificity of psychoanalysis is its location within a field of representation. My objection to that is we cannot deny psychology the right to use a heuristic series which is the prerogative of many other sciences: imaginary, hypothesis, verification. The reduction of psychology to a reality without truth, to a sort of unthinking empiricism appears to be the price that has to be paid (by the other, by psychology!) in order to consolidate the autonomy of the psychoanalytic field. This reductionism becomes strikingly obvious in another passage (Green, 1979, p. 41) which claims to differentiate between psychoanalysis and psychology on the basis of their respective methods, rather than their objects:

> We have to choose between, on the one hand, the sensible and, on the other, the imaginable and the deducible, even though that distinction no longer holds at the conceptual level as the 'pure' sensible no longer exists. Let us say that we have to choose between the limitations imposed by objectification, and the inevitable 'supplement' that is introduced by the basic heuristic hypothesis. Ultimately, the former approach, which claims to be rigorous, has nothing to say because it is unwilling to make inferences; at any event, if it is to be consistent, it must abandon the attempt to understand the psychical representative. The second attitude, which takes the representative as its object, lucidly admits to being conjectural on the grounds that the representative is, by definition, conjectural. The specificity of the representative resides precisely in the fact that it is not constrained by the restrictive demands of the real, that its essential quality is to bring about the possible by means of the workings of the psyche alone.

The expulsion of psychology and the return of panpsychoanalyticism

The distinction between the psychological approach and the psychoanalytic appoach should, then, be couched in terms of a triple opposition: in pychology we have the sensible, objectification and non-inference; in psychoanalysis we have the imaginable, the deducible, basic heuristic hypotheses and the psychical representative as object. But what psychologist of any school would accept the option of non-inference, objectification and the pure sensible? What child psychologist would reject hypotheses, the imaginary and deduction, or even the use of the term 'representative', at least as a hypothetical construct? If we claim that the former approach has no scientific content, in the sense that it has no truth content, we are in fact claiming that psychoanalysis is the only science and giving it exclusive rights over the latter option, heuristic hypotheses and deduction included. Although Green is attempting to make a distinction between the two domains, and I am quite in agreement with him there, he therefore reduces the domain of 'psychology' to being a shadow, or, which amounts to the same thing, to a pure empiric. Does not this mark the *return of psychoanalyticism*? The effects of Freud's reductionism are still present. Green says that psychoanalysis is conjectural, but the term is ambiguous. If it means that its object (the 'representative') is a construct, a supposition which is not directly accessible to observation, the same could be said of *any* science. But if we say that the representative is 'not constrained by the restrictive demands of the real', and that its 'essential quality is to bring about the possible', we become involved in a very different argument which concerns the human being's capacity for self-symbolization. We then have to admit that psychoanalysis, *like all knowledge*, works with hypotheses, conjectures and representatives, its specificity being that it takes as its object the human subject *in so far as* that subject is auto-hypothetical, auto-conjectural, auto-representative or auto-theorizing. The issue of the distinction — and the relationship — between the two levels of theoretization is obviously problematical, but conflating them is clearly out of the question.

The psychology of the infant: a minimal but real basis for psychoanalysis

Fortunately, in my view, an understanding of the origins of human consciousness is being developed on the basis of observation, despite psychoanalysis's attempts to annexe it, infiltrate it and cut it down to size. I say 'fortunately' because our object here is to trace the emergence or genesis of sexuality. Psychoanalytic knowledge provides us with some new insights, but if we are to attain that object, we require certain minimal foundations. As we overcome our fear of putting forward arguments and formulating hypotheses and conjectures, both the early approximations of the psychoanalystis and the more or less justifiable rationalizations of psychologists like Piaget begin to give way to a much more detailed understanding of how the young child relates to the world and the environment, animate and inanimate, part or whole, and, in a word, of the evolution and development of sensori- or perceptive-motor patterns that go to make up the 'equipment' of the infant, even if it is — as I still believe — a minimal equipment. Child psychology has been able to develop without the contradictory hypothesis of primary narcissism, even if it does feel that it has to make the occasional bow to what it assumes to be psychoanalysis. Lagache had already begun to outline this description of the young human being when he denounced what he called 'rash assertions' about non-differentiation.

Lagache's programme

The notion of primary differentiation is preferable to the more commonly adopted notion of non-differentiation. Non-differentiation [between the infant and its environment] is

relative to later stages; it is not absolute, as might be implied
by certain rash formulations as to the absence of consciousness,
the absence of the subject, of the object and therefore of
object-relations. The existence of primary differentiation is
indicated by the existence of apparatuses which guarantee the
subject a minimal autonomy: the apparatuses of perception,
motricity, memory, thresholds and the discharge of needs and
affects. These apparatuses serve to gratify the drives, and
they are also the first guarantors that the subject is adjusting
to its environment; they exist before any conflict arises, and
they can participate in conflict as independent factors [and
here we find one of Lagache's most precious comments on the
supposed absence of consciousness in the infant, on its supposed
non-differentiation]. To claim that a new-born infant has no
conscious experience of anything is to fly in the face of the
facts, as it alternates between waking and sleeping [and if it
lived in a purely narcissistic state, with sleep as its prototype,
what would that alternation mean?] These conscious experiences are primarily experiences of bodily states and acts; in
other words they are based primarily upon inter- and proprio-
ceptive inputs. The infant is not, however, a prisoner of their
subjectivity. It is difficult to see the new-born infant's relationship with the breast as being anything other than a
subject–object relationship: although it does not exist as a
cognitive structure, the subject does function, and it gradually
becomes a reality as successive needs awaken it and motivate
it, as acts of orientation and then consumption soothe it and
send it to sleep; similarly, breast and milk fulfil an object-
function long before the infant has any positional awareness
of them as objects. (Lagache,1961, pp. 200–1)

Lagache is obviously influenced by the *most positive elements* in
phenomenology, even though he does not use phenomenological jargon: the fact that there is no 'thetic' consciousness
of either object or subject does not necessarily mean that
there is no subject–object relationship, or no non-thetic
consciousness.

Let me make myself quite clear: we seem to be being torn
between two ineluctable and mutually exclusive totalitarian-

isms: the totalitarianism of the 'mythical' psychoanalytic child (and as I have already stated, I find the term 'mythical' highly dubious), and that of the observable psychological child who is the object of scientific constructs. The problem is that both these claimants to hegemony in fact intersect or rather overlap, as do self-preservation and sexuality. So much so that both psychoanalysis's 'mythical child' and psychology's child are in a sense abstractions. But there is no denying that they imply different approaches.

Observation and inference in psychology and in psychoanalysis

We often hear it said that the psychoanalytic child is a product of the experimental situation which defines it, and it is well known that it is an artificial situation. It is only within the analytic situation, or the situation of child analysis, that we have access to the psychoanalytic child. Yet between the experimental situation and the analytic situation, there lies a no man's land, a public domain. This is the realm of observation, and observation can focus either on the major apparatuses and on adaptation, or on the birth of the 'psychoanalytic' in a spontaneous relationship; and this is precisely what Melanie Klein does in her 'On Observing the Behaviour of Young Infants' (Klein, 1952a).

The importance of psychoanalytic observation therefore cannot be denied. We also have Freud's observations of the *fort-da* game; but unlike his observations of 'Little Hans', that observation was not made within a psychoanalytic situation. The difference between psychoanalytic and psychological observation is not the fact that one is indirect and that the other is direct Both are indirect in that no observation worthy of the name is devoid of hypotheses, and hypotheses require indirect verification. But I would stress that psychoanalytic observation is indirect in two senses. Firstly, it is indirect in that any attempt to know or cognize is indirect; secondly, its object is 'indirect'. In order to make that point, we have only to introduce the notion of time and the dimen-

sion which gives it its specificity within psychoanalysis: deferred action. Deferred action is a two-stage mechanism, and
neither of its stages can be detected on its own. It is possible
to trace the development of perception step by step, even
though it does involve phenomena such as breaks, changes of
function and repetition. If it is true to say that *it always takes
two traumas to make a trauma*, or two distinct events to produce
repression, then it is also true to say that primary represion,
or trauma, is not something that can be pinpointed thanks to
observation, even if the observer is a psychoanalyst. Analytic
observers are fated to being either too early or too late, not
because some ill-defined metaphysical curse has been laid
upon them, but because their object itself is constructed in
two stages. Analytic processes can, by definition, only be
delineated within a framework. One of the most successful
attempts to do so is, in my view, Sylvia Bleichmar's study of
the origins of the psychical subject in clinical child psychoanalysis (Bleichmar, 1985, p.9), where she attempts to
delineate a clinical framework for certain basic theoretical
hypotheses:

> Mythical periods are not constructions, but real moments in
> the structuration of the psychical subject; even if we do not
> succeed in apprehending them in their subjectivity, we can
> delineate them in the same way that we can delineate an
> element in Mendeleyev's periodic table...Even though we
> can neither see it nor touch it, we do know its specific weight,
> its density, its effect and how it combines with other elements.

3

Foundations: Towards a General Theory of Seduction

The whole of chapter 2 was devoted to an epistemological spring-cleaning, to a mine-sweeping operation (and some of the mines were laid by Freud himself). I have tried to account for the fact that, when all the commentaries are over and done with, there comes a moment when it is possible to opt for one Freud rather than the other to the extent that it is possible to find a real explanation of how Freud was led astray by his object.

So we come to our 'new foundations', to basics which might also be described as 'primals': it should now be clear that for me the primal is neither an abstract category, a philosophical transcendental nor a timeless 'myth'. And nor is it a 'mythical time', as myths are in fact quite fond of travelling through fictional time, whereas we are dealing with real time. For me, and for Freud as it happens, the primal is that element in the initial situation which is inevitable, which is beyond even the most general contingency. And here we do of course have to take into account the difference between the category of universality and that of generality. Socrates is mortal because all men are essentially mortal, and dealing with the primal means dealing with the universal.

3.1 The primal situation: adult−child

The *primal situation* is one in which a new-born child, an

infant in the etymological sense of the word (*in-fans*: speechless), is confronted with the adult world. This may even mean that what we call the Oedipus complex is in a sense subject to contingency. At this point we can turn for help to anthropology, and to the way it relativizes oedipal structures. We can also turn to futurology. After all, what will remain of the classic Oedipal triangle — not triangulation — in a few decades, or a few hundred years? Is anyone prepared to bet on the survival of the Oedipus on which Freud bases his arguments? Is anyone prepared to claim that human beings will cease to be human beings if it does not survive?

Does going back to fundamentals therefore mean going back to the most universal thing of all, namely the mother—child relationship? As we know, psychoanalysis does tend to work backwards from the Oedipal relationship to the mother—child relationship. And no doubt that relationship is more firmly rooted in the biological — and above all the instinctual, in the sense in which that term will be defined below — than the Oedipus. And yet the mother—child relationship is changing very quickly. Without wishing to look too far into the future, though we should keep it within our peripheral field of vision, it should be recalled that more and more children are being brought into the world by artificial means, whilst the fact that fewer and fewer children ever have any real contact with 'the breast' surely means that we have to question something that psychoanalysts take to be an almost obligatory prototype.

Merleau-Ponty discusses Margaret Mead

I will make a digression here to discuss some of the reading I did while researching this book; while I was working on the notion of a primal situation and on its implications (namely seduction), I reread Merleau-Ponty's summary discussion of Margaret Mead. I am thinking of *Male and Female* (Mead, 1950) and of the lectures given by Merleau-Ponty when he took over the chair in child psychology at the Sorbonne —

they were published in the old *Bulletin de psychologie*. There is something attractive about Merleau-Ponty's gradualist approach and the interest he took in matters which many psychoanalysts regard as being beneath their dignity. I will cite only these few lines in which Merleau-Ponty (1964, p. 120) achieves an even deeper insight than Mead:

> According to Margaret Mead, the oedipal situation described by Freud is no more than a particular solution to what appears to be a universal problem. What is universal [note the use of the term 'universal'] is that the existence of parents and children creates a certain problem for all societies. The *universal fact* is that *children exist*, that they start out *small and weak, but are closely associated with adult life*. We therefore find a 'premature double blooming of sexual feeling in the child unready for procreation' (Mead,1950, p. 127). The child's experience is polarised around sexual questions, but it is at the same time incapable of performing the characteristic activities of an adult.

The text cited by Merleau-Ponty can of course be seen as an expression of 'culturalism' (a term which is, for unknown reasons, currently used in a pejorative sense), or in other words of the way certain psychoanalytic parameters — all psychoanalytic parameters — may vary as a result of cultural differences. The sacrosanct universality of the Oedipus can be seen as one of the many solutions to a problem created by the situation in which adults and children relate to one another (and that is universal), and by the entry of the child into the adult universe. Similarly, to take Mead's argument a little further, pregenital sexuality is subject to considerable cultural variation, and so, and that is the point of both the book and the title, is the famous masculinity—femininity pair. And (dare I say it) Freud is, as it happens, in complete agreement with Margaret Mead on this point. He states that the masculinity—femininity pair is simply the belated, complex and unpredictable outcome of a process in which sociological factors play a major role. Culturalism can, then,

go hand in hand with essentialism, or the fact of getting
down to essentials at some point; the two approaches can
complement one another. It will, however, soon become
apparent that, despite her insights, Margaret Mead fails to
see the essential thing about adult—child relations. Not that
that detracts from the value of her observations. What
wouldn't I give for a Margaret Mead who could see into the
future! As it is, we have only an anthropologist who works
with space, with the simultaneous civilizations that are to be
met with on the surface of the globe.

My second digression is intended to point out how much
we can learn from Merleau-Ponty's lecture notes. A
philosopher who is willing to observe! A philosopher
interested in clinical observation, in very concrete
experiments involving children, and in the observations of an
anthropologist! He could teach a lesson to more than one
psychoanalyst. We can learn the same lesson from Freud,
who was never afraid to refer to observation, and to
anthropological observation in particular. A self-confident
psychoanalysis should be able to adopt the approach of all
great thinkers; it must overcome its snobbish attitude to non-
psychoanalytic observation and, if it does want to make use
of it, or if it does want to criticize it, as both Freud and
Merleau certainly did, it must first get over its tendency to
reject it out of hand.

3.2 The Protagonists in the Primal Situation

To return to the primal situation, or the adult—child situation,
which lies as far beyond the Oedipus as it lies beyond the
mother—child relationship. To take the *child* first. Our initial
exercise in catharsis exorcized, among other things, the 'narcissistic' child (that false psychoanalytic child), but it leaves
ample room for something that is at once a matter of common
sense, day-to-day observation and, increasingly, the object of
a psychology which has developed greatly over the last few

years. Whether we want to call it experimental psychology, observational psychology or ethology is largely irrelevant. My aim is not to summarize its findings, but simply to say that it has won its spurs. There is a place for it, provided that we are willing to put psychoanalysis in its proper place. It is rather embarrassing to have to say it, but we are we not in a position to reject in advance the findings of any observation. Some of the findings of day-to-day observation were in fact clearly spelled out by Freud, even though scientific observation has subsequently refined them. I will rapidly summarize what seem to me to be the essential points for our purposes.

A bio-psychical individual . . .

First of all, anyone who talks about a child is by definition talking about a *bio-psychical being*, and the idea that an infant is a pure organism, a pure machine on to which a soul, a psyche or whatever else, has been grafted is an aberration. Anyone who has ever observed a new-born baby knows that its behaviour has a meaning and, what is more important, that it can communicate. After all, why shouldn't it be able to; animal psychology manages perfectly well without the old body—soul problem which led to so much confusion. The only question worth asking about bio-psychical or somato-psychical individuals is this: at what point does communication begin? But that rapidly becomes a complex question, as we immediately have to make a hierarchical distinction between different types of communication.

. . . aware of the world . . .

My second point has already been explored at some length in the previous chapter: for the young human being *the problem of becoming aware of or open to is a false problem;* the only thing that is problematical is closure: the closure of a self or an ego, whatever the circumference or periphery of that ego may be. And we know that a periphery has, as it were, several perimeters, that its geometry can vary, so much so that I habitually invert the terms of Winnicott's famous 'first not-me possession' (Winnicott, 1953) by saying that the real problem is, rather, one of acquiring a 'first-me possession', of acquiring a sense of self.

Once again, Freud provides us with certain clues, especially in the *Project for a Scientific Psychology* (Freud, 1950, p. 326 ff.), where it is the question of closure that is raised rather than that of openness. It will be recalled that, in the *Project*, there is *too much* perceptive reality. Everything is real, and a so-called 'indication of reality' has to be found so as to distinguish between what is and what is not real about that reality, rather as though the real world, as opposed to the world of fantasy, the imaginary or the non-real, were marked by a supplementary sign. This is of course a naïve question, and Aristotle raises the obvious objection: if reality has to be indicated, what indicates the indication? If reality has to be marked, how are we to recognize its mark? In fact Freud is not satisfied with the idea of an indication of reality, and argues that it is thanks only to inhibition that a subjective world can be carved out from the whole of perceptive reality. It is only because certain a type of process originating inside the system is inhibited, and because its intensity is reduced — and this a purely quantitative and non-qualitative mechanism — that a distinction can be made between the two.

Staying with Freud, we find another clue in the recently published *Overview of the Transference Neuroses*. We have already seen that, in this text, Freud (1987, p. 9) explicitly relates the symptomatology of anxiety neurosis — with its so-called hypnoid or oniroid states, in which the distinction between dream and reality is no longer marked — to regression to a 'phase without separation of Pcs and Ucs', to a phase without speech and censorship, as it is indeed speech and censorship which introduce the distinction between the pre-conscious — consciousness system and the unconscious system. It follows that, if we accept the existence of a phase without separation of Pcs and Ucs, we must then ask what kind of phase it is. Two apparently simple answers come to mind. Either it is totally unconscious, or it is totally conscious (or pre-conscious). It also follows that origins are unconscious, that the infant lives in something known as the unconscious, or something that will become the unconscious and will be delineated or circumscribed by the famous fence around the 'nature reserve', that will be confined to the ghetto of the unconscious. This is obviously what Freud is actually saying, even if, as I do, we reject his argument. In the *Project,* this idea is bound up with the notion that it is in fact language which introduces consciousness and that, prior to the existence of language, we have unconsciousness. This is, however, highly debatable, even in Freudian terms. There is more justification for thinking that there is initially something of the order of a consciousness, a presence in the world, or a sort of conscious—preconscious system. It will be recalled that Freud originally left ample room for just this kind of primal conscious-perception system, for a system which, unlike secondary consciousness, was non-verbal.

To go back to the infant. This interpretation, which rejects the idea of a primal unconscious, is quite in keeping with the basic findings of the most impartial observer. It is also in keeping with Lagache's extremely important remark to the effect that, from birth onwards, we observe an alternation between presence and non-presence, and how can there be non-presence, or sleep, if there is no presence? If there is indeed a prototype, in the sense of Freud's *Vorbild,* for the 'first-me possession', to parody Winnicott once more, it may well be sleep, or dreams.

Supplied with regulatory patterns . . .

What then is an infant? A set of patterns which physiology and ethology are now able to describe with increasing accuracy. In the absence of proof to the contrary, the basic pattern is still homeostasis, or the tendency to maintain, or return to, a level of equilibrium. Homeostasis can be detected at two levels: at a specifically physiological level, and at the psychological or instinctual level. At the first level, we find in the infant and in human beings in general, biological constants including, to take the simplest examples, a constant level of substances such as carbon dioxide and glucose in the blood. All those constants are regulated by feedback mechanisms which are now well known. It must, however, be recalled that, in the infant, these physiological constants are imperfect; it is only gradually that they become stabilized, as we know that an infant can die of heatstroke and that, unless we are very attentive, it can become dehydrated without anyone noticing. At a second level, we find patterns which are of greater interest to us, even though they are grafted on to the former level. We can, that is, observe adaptational forms of behaviour in infants, even though adaptation does not explain everything. We are, for example gradually acquiring a better understanding of the pre-consumption or consumption patterns that lead up to suckling. At this level of adaptation, we cannot ignore the existence of perceptive-motor schemata which allow us to trace the development of what simply has to be called attention, habits, memory, and so on. This growing body of knowledge contradicts both the notion that the infant is a closed organism (I was about to say an amoeba...but an amoeba is not a closed organism) and the notion that it is a *tabula rasa* with no directional vectors. If, that is, homeostatic mechanisms are to be found in the infant, it must have 'values' and it is very tempting to follow Lagache in decribing them as 'life values' and to say that they allow an equilibrium to be re-established.

But ill-equipped

An infant is neither a closed system nor a *tabula rasa*, but it is very poorly adapted to its environment. The term 'prematuration' is, quite rightly, still in use, and can be defined as follows: the fact of being faced with tasks which are too complex

for an individual who has reached a given degree of physiological maturation. But in the case of the young human
being, a distinction has to be made between two different
types of prematuration precisely because we have to make a
distinction between the level of self-preservation and the
sexual level. In terms of adaptation, prematuration is bound
up with the problem of survival; in the sexual domain, prematuration refers to the fact that the infant is confronted with a
sexuality to which it has, to quote Margaret Mead,no adequate response. What Freud calls the presexual state will later
be discussed at some length. For the moment, I would like to
return to the question of prematuration in the domain of
survival. Human beings are not the only creatures to need
help from adults if they are to survive; prematuration is not
the sole explanation of how an infant becomes a human being,
and nor is it a complete explanation. Other mammals and
some non-mammalians also need to be helped and educated
for variable periods of time. Even some baby birds have to be
fed in the nest; not all baby birds are like chickens, which
begin to peck around for food as soon as they emerge from
the egg. From the outset, Freud uses the term *Hilflosigkeit* to
define this need for help or absence of help.

Die Hilflosigkeit

The term is difficult to translate, but it is not difficult to
understand what it means. In German it has in a way an
affective charge, and suggests 'distress' (and in French it is
sometimes translated as *détresse*) or even 'abandonment'. It
has to be said, however, that its affective connotations are
much weaker in Freud than in the German language as a
whole. The term connotes a very objective state, and it is
unfortunate that no real French equivalent has been found :
the expression designates a helpless condition (*état sans aide*)
or a distressful state (*état d'insecours*). *Hilflosigkeit* refers, in a
word, to the state of a being which, when left to its own
devices, is incapable of helping itself, and which therefore

needs help from others (Freud uses the expression *fremde Hilfe*). We find references to this need for help from others in the opening sections of the *Project*. How does the small human machine known as the primary psychical apparatus call upon others for help? It does so purely because it is overwhelmed by excitation stemming from within. Left to itself, it is incapable of triggering the mechanisms which would allow it to establish a new equilibrium; if one's blood sugar level is low, the only remedy is to go and look for a piece of bread, but a young infant is not capable of going to look for milk. It cannot call out or send messages, and therefore has to use simple objective indications to ask for help. Eventually, the pot boils over: it cries and kicks and shouts, and its mother very quickly learns to recognize that this is a cry for help. Whilst Freud's complete refusal to admit that there is any preadapted channel of communication between mother and child is open to criticism, certain of his notions are still highly suggestive. I am thinking particularly of the idea that, at the level of self-preservation or adaptation (I am using the terms interchangeably), the channel of communication goes from child to parent, whereas the reverse is true in the sexual domain. The child, that is, evolves from adaptation to sexuality, but Freud unhesitatingly states that in her relationship with the child, a mother moves from sexuality to affection: 'A mother's love for the infant she suckles and cares for is something far more profound than her later affection for the growing child' (Freud, 1910a, p. 117). Mother and child take very different paths.

I said a moment ago that *Hilflosigkeit* must not be reduced to meaning panic or abandonment. The child's inability to help itself is not restricted to the search for positive values such as subsistence, food and drink; it also comes into play at the level of avoiding danger, or in other words in what is known as the fright reaction. Freud does make this point, and it is interesting to note that his comments have been substantiated by more recent experiments. In the *Introductory Lectures*, Freud (1916–17, p. 408) tells us to look at children:

they run along the brink of the water, climb on the window sill, play with sharp objects and fire. They have no notion of danger, no sense of fear. Children are fearless because they have no instinct to adapt; in a sense a child is *hilflos* in this area too simply because it needs help from others but does not realize the fact. The results of day-to-day observation can be scientifically confirmed by experiments on reactions to danger. The behaviour of a young child faced with a void can be compared with that of a young bird belonging to a species which normally nests in holes in cliffs. It is a simple experiment: a completely transparent sheet of glass is placed over a hole and the subject is placed on the glass. The baby steps forward as though nothing were wrong, whereas the bird refuses to walk out over the void. A simple experiment in observation shows quite conclusively that the young human being is helpless in the face of danger, or even unable to perceive danger.

Realistic Anxiety: a long debate

This major observation is inscribed within what Freud himself calls the 'long debate' (1987, p. 14) that continues throughout his theory. Which is the earlier: what Freud terms *Realangst* (realistic anxiety) or *Triebangst* (literally 'instinctual anxiety'). In other words, which appears first in human beings: fear ('realistic anxiety' is, ultimately, fear; the German term *Angst* covers both) or an anxiety reaction to an attack by an internal drive, an 'instinctual anxiety'? The latter is not even a 'reaction to'; it does not come after the danger because in *Triebangst* there is no time interval between danger and fear or the perception of danger. When a drive is concerned, the threat of danger is *in itself* a form of anxiety. Freud constantly oscillates between the two conceptions, as he himself notes in the *Overview of the Transference Neuroses*. In the course of this 'long debate', he first gives priority and, so to speak, psycho-analytic pride of place, to 'instinctual anxiety' or *Sehnsuchtangst*, a related term which can be translated as 'anxiety of longing'.

We psychoanalysts tend to take the same view, and to see anxiety of longing as appearing before realistic anxiety; this is quite in keeping with the above remarks on the helplessness of the young child who has no innate knowledge of danger and no instinctual intuition of its existence. To quote from the text of the Overview (1987, p.14)

> Now we see in infantile anxiety that, when satisfaction is denied [this is still a mechanist view; the ego is overwhelmed by libido], the child transforms the object-libido into realistic anxiety about strangers, but we also see that it is generally inclined to be fearful of anything new.[17] We have carried on a long debate over whether realistic anxiety or anxiety of longing is the earlier of the two; whether the child changes his libido into realistic anxiety because he regards [it] as too great, dangerous, and thus arrives at an idea of danger, or whether he rather yields to a general anxiousness and learns from this also to be afraid of his unsatisfied libido.

The psychoanalytic consensus definitely supports the view that anxiety is an internal process : the ego comes under attack from the drive. But at this point, Freud arbitrarily tips the scales in the opposite direction by introducing another form of 'realistic anxiety', and by appealing to phylogenesis (1987, p.14):

> Now phylogenetic consideration seems to settle this dispute in favour of realistic anxiety and permits us to assume that a portion of the children bring along the anxiousness of the beginning of the Ice Age and are now induced by it to treat the unsatisfied libido as an external danger.

Freud is once more looking for exogenous foundations which are extrinsic to psychoanalysis. He now refers to the men of the Ice Age that came after the age of the primeval paradise. We have already criticized this appeal to arbitrary foundations, but this is not simply another appeal to the instinctual: the atavism that is acquired in this way has nothing to do with learning about specific dangers or with the ability to react appropriately (as would a young animal); on the contrary, this is a truly *pathological and non-adaptational development*: a general tendency to be anxious to fear anything new — even the appearance of 'longing' — to see it as a threat and to treat it as such.

This discussion of the precise meaning of *Hilflosigkeit* was intended to provide a better introduction to one of the protagonists in the primal or fundamental situation by exorcizing the ghost of prehistory. Although the child is not without certain patterns and a certain ability to adapt, and although we are beginning to understand it more clearly, it is (without wishing to strike a note of pathos) still basically doomed to *Hilflosigkeit*; it must necessarily receive help from others both to satisfy its needs and to ward off danger until such time as it learns to be afraid. The child has no natural sense of fear; fear is something which is learned, and not from experience alone. We can be taught to be afraid; we do not keep away from fire because we have touched it, but quite simply because we have been told not to.

The adult as protagonist

We can now turn to the other protagonist: the adult. We know that Ferenczi (1933) uses the expression 'language of passion' to characterize the 'adult world', but it seems to me that he overlooks the major coordinate: the unconscious of the adult. A few exceptional passages aside, Freud too tends to overlook the problem of the adult unconscious and, more generally, that of the unconscious of the other. But, as always, the exceptions are of great help to us. Two are of particular relevance. In 'The Taboo of Virginity' (Freud, 1918a) the taboo of virginity is seen as being based upon a perception of the other's unconscious wish (the wish to be castrated by a woman or by one's mother), and in *Leonardo* Freud (1910a, p. 117) quite specifically alludes to the fact that a mother's love for her child is a way of satisfying her repressed wishful impulses.

The dimension of the unconscious

We have, then, an adult, and the dimension of the unconscious. For the moment, we can forget about theories about the essence of the unconscious and look at the psychoanalytic discovery before it has been theorized in terms of either the first topography (repression and the system Ucs) or the second, more complex topography, (the Id). Let us go so far as provisionally to accept an anti-realist conception of the unconscious, that promoted by Politzer (1928) or, in rather more modern form, by the phenomenologists or Schafer (1976). I have adopted this conception on more than one occasion, if only as a debating point, and we can adopt it here, purely in order to establish the primal situation. Let us look, then, at the psychoanalytic discovery at its most demonstrable level, or rather at the level where it is most fit to be seen.

At what level is a non-theorized psychoanalysis fit to be seen? Is it at the level of the dream, of the 'royal road' to the unconscious? Anyone who rereads the *Introductory Lectures* (Freud, 1916—17) cannot fail to be struck by the fact that they begin, not with dreams, but with *Fehlleistungen*, a term which we are obliged to translate as 'parapraxes', or bungled actions, though it also covers other actions such as slips of the tongue or slips of the pen. Freud begins with the most revealing and most basic bungled action, the slip of the tongue, and reminds us that a *Leistung*, which refers to the action itself, is intended to communicate something even before it is bungled. What is more important, it is the fact of its being bungled that has a sense. It always conveys something which has been repressed, and the repressed element may exist at a number of different levels. Freud distinguishes between three different levels, depending on how the subject reacts to the psychoanalyst's interpretation: at one level, the subject accepts the meaning that is suggested but takes the view that it is irrelevant. At another level, it takes a certain amount of work to make the subject accept the meaning. And finally, at a third level, the subject completely refuses to accept the meaning proposed by the psychoanalyst. The three levels correspond to the depth of the repression, but the important point is that a sense has been detected and that it was not visible to the individual who conveyed it at the precise moment when he conveyed it. The human being is, then, described as being capable of making slips of the tongue and of performing bungled actions. It would be interesting to know whether animals are capable of bungled actions (in Freud's sense of that term). We know — or think — that animals are capable of dreaming, as we can see reactions which appear to be reactions to dreams, and it would also be interesting to know from observation the age at which a child is capable of performing a bungled action. A bungled action bears witness, then, to the fact that there is 'something unconscious',[18] to the fact that there are messages which the subject rejects or refuses to recognize for what they are.[19]

In the primal situation we have, then, a child whose ability to adapt is real but limited, weak and waiting to be perverted, and a deviant adult (deviant with regard to any sexual norms, as Freud demonstrates more than adequately in the *Three Essays*; for my part I would add that the adult is deviant or split with regard to himself). One further detail should be added: given that the child lives on in the adult, an adult faced with a child is particularly likely to be deviant and inclined to perform bungled or even symbolic actions because he is involved in a relationship with his other self, with the other he once was. The child in front of him brings out the child within him. The primal relationship is therefore established on a twofold register: we have both a vital, open and reciprocal relationship, which can truly be said to be interactive, and a relationship which is implictly sexual, where there is no interaction because the two partners are not equal. In human beings, actions are not always equal to reactions, as physics would have it. Here, we have seducer and seduced, perverter and perverted. Someone is moving away from the straight and narrow; we have here a 'Traviata', someone who has been led astray and 'seduced'.

3.3 From the special theory of seduction to the general theory of seduction

We now come to the heart of our 'new foundations for psychoanalysis', to seduction as the major generative factor in psychoanalysis. It is a generative factor at several different levels, operating both at the initial level of childhood and at the level of psychoanalytic practice. We will have to define it more precisely, but for the moment we need to look briefly at the history of Freud's thought. We will, however, do so in broad, schematic terms, as our concern is with the current foundations of psychoanalysis.

In both Freud's thought and contemporary thought, seduction is always a link between a *factuality*, meaning facts or an effective reality, and a certain *theorization* of those facts. Facts and theorization are intimately bound up with one another. They appear and disappear together. Table 3.1 illustrates my point.

Situating Freud

In a sense, the centre column of table 3.1 is a summary of Freud, and it is obviously rather foolhardy to speak of the whole of Freud's thought having been repressed; nevertheless, the constraints of repression never stopped anything from existing, or even from progressing. I will use what is, ultimately, a negative assessment to make the point that there are always two alternatives open to us when we approach any great author (and not only Freud) in an attempt to trace the history of his thought or his heritage. We can either situate the author, and leave it at that, which is one way of doing him justice. But to do so also means doing him an injustice, because we tend to restrict his thought

Table 3.1

21 September 1897	1964–67	
Factuality		
Childhood seduction	Precocious seduction	Primal seduction
Theory		
Special theory	Repression and break-up of theory	General theory
Temporal aspect	Isolated (deferred action)	Temporal aspect
Topographical aspect	Evolves separately (topographies)	topographical aspect
Language aspect, 'translation'	Disappears	Language aspect metabola
	Reduction and confusion of levels (self-preservation and sexuality)	
	Substitute formations biologism of drive phylogenesis of fantasies	
Theory of cure (complete dominance of conscious over unconscious)	Theory of cure (transference as illusion)	Theory of cure (transcendence of transference

to his actual words. The alternative is to bring out and expand the most advanced elements, or what we see as the most advanced elements, in his thought. I normally adopt the second alternative: when I am discussing Freud, I usually concentrate on what is best in him in an attempt to find inspiration. But this is why, on the other hand, I think it is from time to time legitimate, or even essential, to take him literally and to look at what he actually intended to say. It was, after all, Freud himself who spoke of having abandoned the seduction theory.

Table 3.1 spares us the need for a full commentary, as the central section, which is headed 'Repression of theory', was to a large extent the subject matter of our first 'cathartic' chapter. Without claiming to be a historian, I will begin by looking at the first panel in the triptych or at what I call the special theory of seduction, and will then go on to discuss the transition from infantile seduction to precocious and then primal seduction. I will begin, that is, by looking at the 'factuality' column. Finally, I will discuss the right-hand column, which seems to me to represent the modern contribution.

Freud's special theory of seduction has both its strengths and its weaknesses. Both stem from the close interweave between the factuality of seduction and the complexities of the theory; if a few stitches in the fabric give, it is possible that it will fall apart completely. The factuality identified at this time is what I call 'infantile seduction', and it takes the concrete form of scenes which can, thanks to the analytic method, be rediscovered, reconstructed and remembered. But as we know, Freud, both in this period and in later stages of his work, has no qualms about intercutting intra-analytic reminiscences with information derived from other people, and sometimes even makes real objective investigations. All his writings from this period abound in examples of events reflecting what he calls 'premature sexual experience', (1896b, p. 203), of events in which a young child is passively confronted with the irruption of adult sexuality. The child involved in what we can define as an 'infantile' seduction is always immature, and is unable to respond adequately to what happens to it. In certain texts, Freud (1896b, p.212) traces these memories back to 'even the second year of life', but the real issue is one of the interval between events rather than pure chronology. It is the interval that is the breeding ground for trauma. A comparison could be drawn here with traumatic neurosis in adults, where the essential feature of the trauma relates to the fortuitous character of the accident, to the fact that the subject was not prepared for it: the child's lack of preparedness is basically synonymous with its *Hilflosigkeit* or, as Freud puts it here (p. 213), with 'a certain *infantile* state of the psychical functions, as well as of the sexual system'. The accident or event that occurs appears to be arbitrary, just as it does in adult traumatic neurosis. Immaturity or 'the sexual impotence which is inherent in children', to cite Freud (1896b, p. 215), must be evaluated on the basis of a sort of scale of development comprising stages separated by thresholds: levels of somatic reaction, levels of affective reaction and levels of psychical or intellectual understanding, all go together. It is at the level of its whole psycho-somato-affective existence that the child can or cannot adequately integrate what happens to it. The major threshold of puberty serves as a model for these thresholds; in terms of later psychoanalytic descriptions, it is a relatively late stage, but it does prefigure other thresholds and, of course, the later notion of stages. The 'presexual' stage we are discussing is therefore both an absolute and relative 'pre-': it exists 'before' a certain type of understanding is possible, and the 'presexual' can take different forms corresponding to the different stages in the evolution of the child.

A perverse adult

The second important feature of these scenes is that the partner in the seduction is inevitably an *adult*. It is vital to note how Freud deals with cases which appear to be an exception to the rule and in which the sexual scene that is recalled takes place between two children or two adolescents.

When the scene involves two children, Freud regularly claims
to be able to go back to a more archaic scene in which one of
the two children (and perhaps both) has suffered an 'infection
in childhood' (infection is Freud's term, (1896b, p. 209); he
sometimes uses *Uebertragung*, meaning transmission and transference): 'When the relation is between two children, the
character of the sexual scenes is none the less of the same
repulsive sort, since every such relationship between children
postulates a previous seduction of one of them by an adult'
(1896b, p. 215) [my italics].

The adult involved is not, however, just any adult: it is
always a *perverse* adult. The word has to be understood in its
strong sense, in the twofold sense it will acquire in the *Three
Essays on the Theory of Sexuality* (Freud, 1905), in other words
as meaning deviant in relation to both object and aim. The
object is deviant precisely because the adult is a paedophile,
or even commits incest; the aim is deviant because (1896b,
p. 214): 'People who have no hesitation in satisfying their
sexual desires upon children cannot be expected to jib at
finer shades in the methods of obtaining that satisfaction.'
The whole passage from which this quotation is drawn describes the 'grotesque', repulsive, and 'tragic incongruities' of
sexual relations between 'the ill-matched pair', (p. 215) in
terms of which Nabokov would not be ashamed. Until the
moment when he rejects the whole of his theory (in September
1897), Freud continues to insist upon the perverse character
of the figure he describes in schematic terms as the 'father of
the hysteric'. The scenes in question are openly described as
pathological, and their *pathological* character has a lot to do
with the impasse in which Freud finds himself. Although we
have mentioned the *Three Essays*, it must not be forgotten that
they had yet to be written; it is only with the *Three Essays* that
Freud will introduce the notion of perversion by demonstrating
that the *whole development of sexuality* is marked by the absence
of a predetermined aim and object and that, whilst the whole
of sexuality cannot be said to be perverse in a clinical sense,

it is only after a long period of wandering that the subject
reaches the stage of so-called genital sexuality. The central
theme of the *Three Essays* is that aims are precarious and
interchangeable, and that the 'lost' object is both alien and
inaccessible. Unfortunately 'the father of the hysteric' does
not enjoy the benefit of a theoretical perspective which would
have given him a place within human evolution as a whole.
Such is intellectual history.

A sequence of scenes

Freud speaks (1896b, p. 203) of 'one or more occurrences',
but in practice all his clinical examples deal with several
related events or several overlapping scenes which form a
temporal sequence and which, and this is more important,
symbolize one another. At first sight, we do of course find an
overall analogy within this inter-symbolization of scenes: the
scenarios may be similar and may refer to one another, but
the important point is that, if we compare these scenes element
by element, a more complex metabolism emerges over and
beyond the overall analogy, and that it is precisely the same
kind of metabolism which Freud detects between a dream
and latent dream-thoughts or, perhaps, between a dream
and a scene that took place the previous day. The figure
which is used to illustrate the Emma case in the *Project*
(Freud, 1950, p. 354) is very similar to those used to describe
dreams. It is of course possible that there may be an overall
analogy, as in dreams, but that is much less important than
the extremely complex intersection of one-to-one correspon-
dences based upon contiguity, similarity and difference.

One scene masks another, and in its turn the second scene
suggests the existence of a third. It is that which stimulates
the 'drive to know' that inspires Freud. He works backwards
from scene to scene, and finally reaches an improbable first
scene, the true primal scene; and it is the improbability or
absence of that scene which will provide the key to all the

others and which will clinch the argument during the crisis of 1897. For the moment, let us simply note the apparent aporia posed by these scenes, which constantly refer back to one another in an endless relationship of symbolization: αναγχη στηναι.

The essential passivity of the child

The second feature of the factuality of infantile seduction is the more important, as it is this which defines seduction itself: the relationship of *passivity*, the passivity of the child faced with the adult. It is the adult who takes the initiative in the scenes described by Freud, and who makes advances, either in word or deed; seduction is described in terms of aggression, irruption, intrusion and violence. But this general statement that the adult is active and the child passive has to be qualified in a number of ways, precisely because of the temporal sequence of the scenes. The first qualification (and they all have similar implications) is that Freud (1896a, p. 168) draws a contrast between hysteria, where the child's passivity seems to be an obvious element in its memories, and the aetiology of obsessional neurosis [*Zwangneurose*; the prefix *Zwang* is usually rendered as compulsion; tr.], where 'it is no longer a question of sexual *passivity*, but of acts of aggression carried out with pleasure and of pleasurable participation in sexual acts — that is to say, of sexual *activity*'. If matters were left at that, the seduction theory would apply only to hysteria, whereas anxiety neurosis would originate in scenes involving activity on the part of the child. The opposition in fact breaks down very quickly, as this is in Freud's view a false symmetry: there is no direct correlation between infantile activity and passivity and the two major forms of neurosis, as the activity that is discovered in the obsessional's childhood is always based upon the substratum of an earlier passive experience. If we work backwards from the active scene brought up, so to speak, by the obsessional, we find the passive scene on which it is based: 'In all my cases of obsessional neurosis, moreover, I have found a *substratum of hysterical symptoms* which could be traced back to a scene of sexual passivity that preceded the pleasurable action' (Freud, 1896a, pp. 168–9).

Let us look more closely at this sequence of scenes; as time passes, activity seems to replace passivity, and this is not true of the obsessional alone. In more than one case in which the subject claims to remember having been passively seduced, it can be demonstrated that there was an element of provocation on his or her part. Who is seducing whom? The answer is by no means obvious, and any attempt to arrive at an answer is likely to lead us into a labyrinth of reciprocal interaction, or even a hall of mirrors. After all, the major argument that is put forward against the seduction theory is that children invent fantasies in order to mask their own oedipal wishes, or in other words their own active drives. But in Freud's thought, at least at this time, the explanation is very different: he notes that scenes are actively reproduced, but still claims that they are secondary reworkings of an experience which was predominantly fortuitous and unexpected, and, therefore, of the traumatic aspect and of the child's passivity. To pick up the comparison with the traumatic neurosis of an adult, just as a subject suffering from a neurosis occasioned by an accident reproduces his trauma in his dreams, so the child is, according to this concept of seduction, compelled to repeat scenes actively, to return to the actual scene of the initial outrage, as we can see from the Emma case in the *Project* (Freud, 1950, p. 353–6; cf. Laplanche, 1976, pp. 64 ff.). With the passage of time, the subject becomes more active, and returns more and more frequently to the scene of the event, be it physical or psychical, to relive and revise the trauma.

It will be obvious that the above description of scenes of infantile seduction anticipates what is known as the seduction theory, which I describe as a *special theory*. This theory will be elaborated in three registers, which I will now describe briefly. The three are complementary: the temporal register, the topographical register and the translation register.

The theory: temporal aspect, deferred action

The *temporal* aspect of the seduction theory remains — or at least it is to be hoped that it does — one of psychoanalysis's great assets. I refer to the theory of 'deferred action', to the theory that there are two stages to trauma. This theory postulates that nothing can be inscribed in the human unconscious except in relation to at least two events which are separated from one another in time by a moment of maturation that allows the subject to react in two ways to an initial experience or to the memory of that experience. Freud describes the first moment in terms of fright (*Schreck*) or fright neurosis: the unprepared subject is confronted with a highly meaningful sexual action but cannot take in its significance. If it remains latent, the memory is in itself neither pathogenic nor traumatic. It becomes pathogenic and traumatic when it is revived by a second scene which can be associated with it. But, because the subject can now react in a different way, it is the memory itself, and not the new scene, which functions as a source of traumatic or auto-traumatic energy. Indeed, this two-stage theory shows that it is only because it becomes *auto-traumatic* that a trauma has a pathogenic effect.

Topographical aspect

For reasons pertaining to the second or *topographical* aspect of the process, this auto-traumatic moment cannot be dissolved or worked through by any normal means. It results in the appearance of a 'pathological defence' (or 'repression'; at this stage Freud uses the terms synonymously). Topography becomes the theatre for a whole strategy, in the military sense of the term, and for attack and counter-attack movements. Faced with this sequence of events, the subject is tormented by two kinds of distress. The subject is defenceless or helpless in two senses. During the first attack, which is launched from outside by the adult, or the first sexual scene, it does not have the wherewithal to defend itself; it has no weapons and no answer. At best it may be able to block the enemy's advance and encyst the memory without repressing it. In the second phase, on the other hand, it does have the means to fight back; it can understand what is happening, but finds itself outflanked in this strategic battle; it is attacked at the point where the defences are down. The subject is attacked, that is, from within by a memory and not by an event. Between these two phases, allowance obviously has to be made for the appearance of the *ego*; it is not possible to evade the internal barrier in this way unless the subject-as-totality or the individual-as-totality is supported by the nascent ego: the ego provides the only internal shield against stimuli. At this stage, Freud makes this point in summary terms, but he does make it clearly.

The brilliant thing about this theory is, of course, that it makes nonsense of later attempts to strike a balance between what is exogenous and what is endogenous. Everything is exogenous, but at the same time everything is endogenous; the efficacy of the process stems from the moment of the endogenous reactivation of a memory which obviously derives from a real external event. But the theory of the ego and of its vicissitudes has to be developed — and here it is present only *in nuce* — before it is possible to theorize this topographical aspect, which provides the only radical metapsychological solution to the endless metaphysical debates over the question of inside and outside.

Language and translation

We have dicussed the temporal and the topographical viewpoints, but the seduction theory also develops at a level which
has to be carefully distinguished from the linguistic level: the
level of language and translation. Freud, of course, merely
mentions this in passing and did not even publish his
remarks, which are to be found mainly in his letter of 6
December 1896 to Fliess (Freud, 1985, pp. 207–14), where he
establishes a sequence of scenes and likens relations between
them to a series of 'successive registrations' and transcripts.
Repression is described as a boundary between two epochs of
psychical life and as a partial 'failure of translation'. Many
other points are left unresolved in this letter, notably the
question of how the initial sign or 'indication of perception' is
inscribed in the young human being.

The seduction theory: strengths and weaknesses

Taken as a whole, the theory elaborated by Freud in the
period leading up to September 1897, or the 'special theory
of seduction', has both considerable strengths and certain
weaknesses. Its strengths lie in the way in which the theory is
so closely bound up with data drawn from analytic experience:
the theory is closely intricated with experience. The rigorous
mobilization of the three indissociable factors that go to
make analytic rationality is a further source of strength: the
temporality of deferred action, the topography of the subject
and the intepretative or translation-based links that are established between the scenarios or scenes. Its strengths lie in
the explanatory powers of the model, which is amenable to
transposition and to considerable extension, at least within
the field of psychopathology, and in its capacity to evolve. As
we have already noted, future developments — the notion of
the ego and the tranlsation theory — are already being outlined
here.

Weak points: a theory specific to the psychopathological

The theory's weaknesses, on the other hand, are the weaknesses of any special theory; it tends to be too specific or special-ized. A number of weak points or fault lines can be identified, and they will all give way with the shattering revisions of 21 September 1897. To look first at the scenes themselves, the essence of the phenomenon of seduction is still taken for granted: Freud's conception is restricted to the most obviously psychopathological level, to perverse relations (in the clinical sense) between an adult and a child. Indeed, his clinical conception of perverse relations leads him to raise statistical questions, and rightly so one might think. The argument is as follows: we meet a lot of hysterics in clinical practice; it takes a perverse father to produce a hysteric; but a perverse father is not all it takes to make a hysteric, and other factors must be involved; in statistical terms, it must take 2, 3, n perverse fathers to produce *one* hysteria. If the argument is restricted to the psychopathological features of the fact of seduction and to 'perverse' fathers, there is no escaping this apparently simplistic objection.

The apophantic illusion

At a deeper level, but still in connection with the facts of seduction, Freud fails to see what kind of factuality is involved; to be more specific, he fails to see precisely what mode of reality he is looking for in his analytic investigations. If analytic investigation interprets one scene by means of another, and if there is no meaning to be found other than that revealed by a first apophantic scene ('apophantic' in the sense that the word is applied to the Mysteries), then it is quite obvious that we will never find the hidden scene which reveals all, which is self-explanatory and which does not refer to anything else. Indeed, the search for a first scene which reveals the meaning of the whole sequence will be never-ending and will result in disappointment. The whole question

of what we are looking for in our analytic investigations is at
stake here.[20]

No presentiment of primal repression

We find the same apparent rigidity at the level of theory;
coherent though it may be, the purpose of the model constructed by Freud is to account for the psychopathological,
and the psychopathological alone. Pathological defences,
repression and the unconscious are all part of the same
structure, and the aim of analysis is to break down that
structure: the unconscious is seen as pathological and as
being amenable to reduction by psychoanalysis. The idea of
a 'normal' unconscious which, despite all we know of it, is
irreducible is still out of reach; Freud is not yet able to
postulate the hypothesis of primal repression even though the
seduction theory could explain it. This is why the foolish
hope of 'complete success', of discovering 'the secret of childhood experiences' and of reaching 'the point where the
unconscious is completely tamed by the conscious' (Freud,
1985, pp. 264, 265) inevitably ends in disappointment. But in
his disappointment Freud destroys his theory without further
ado, whereas the relationship between the facts and the
theory could have been completely revitalized if both had
been studied in greater depth. Only a partial and restrictive
aspect of factuality was invoked in the challenge to a theory
which was itself too restrictive, whereas the discussions of
1897 will result in a dialectical reworking of the theory, in a
twofold generalization similar to that which can be observed
elsewhere in the history of the sciences.

3.4   The period of repression

I am gradually coming to what I call the 'general theory of
seduction', which I regard as providing the agenda for the
contemporary period or, to be more specific for the post-

1964—7 period. But we cannot competely ignore the intervening period of 70 years, which accounts for almost the
whole of the invention of psychoanalysis. I describe this
period as one of *repression*, in so far as one can apply the term
'repression' to thought, and to Freud's thought in particular.
The term may, however, have at least some descriptive value
when we are talking about the thought of *one man*, the man
who really created analytic thought. I would not say that we
find the same process of repression in the work of other
authors, or in the work of Freud's heirs and disciples. Their
respect for the master's views induces, rather, a sort of silence,
amnesia or censorship. There is of course the exception of
Ferenczi, and we will return to him later. If we look at
Grinstein's *Index of Psychoanalytic Writings* (Grinstein, 1956—
71), which covers the period up to 1969, the 'key word'
Seduction refers us to a total of four articles by eminently
unknown authors, all of them published in non-psychoanalytic
journals. One of them, which it might be interesting to dig
up, is entitled 'Freud's "Seduction Theory": A Reconstruction'
(Schusdck, 1966), and appeared in what can only be described as a highly specialist publication, namely *The Journal
for the History of Behavioural Sciences*. The others (Kossak, 1913;
Schwarz and Ruggieri, 1959, 1975) are, judging by their
titles, of no more than psychopathological curiosity value, as
they deal with such highly specific questions as the seduction
of children by servants and with the influence of seduction on
criminality.

The theory shattered

In Freud's own post-1987 writings, the seduction theory is
overtaken by a veritable cataclysm. It is shattered, dismemem-
bered and censored. It is then repressed and the remaining
elements undergo a form of secondary revision which makes
then unrecognizable. The central column in table 3.1 tries to
illustrate this. Each element in the seduction theory suffers a
different fate and evolves separately, rather as though it were

trying to find a new context for itself. The 'temporal' or 'deferred action' aspect of the theory, for example, is still an important, even central, theme in psychoanalytic thought, but even that crucial dimension had to be exhumed by Jacques Lacan and his successors. Even so, if we read Freud without any help from Lacan, it is still apparent that deferred action *Nachtraglich*) is still an important Freudian category, especially in a text like the Wolf Man case (Freud, 1918b), where it is of central importance. Jung, however, offers a tempting alternative by objecting that deferred action might be reducible to retrospection pure and simple, action pure and simple. Retrospection, or what Jung calls *Zuruckfantasieren*, simply means the fact of creating a past to meet current needs, perhaps in an attempt to avoid present difficulties and to conceal them from oneself, whereas Freud insists upon the tension between the old scene and the recent scenario. Freud does, however, have difficulty in countering Jung's objecton that the old scene is simply an imaginary and later reconstruction; the only way he can answer that is by postulating an even earlier reality which takes us beyond the limits of individual existence. Pontalis and I describe this tendency at some length in our paper on primal fantasies (Laplanche and Pontalis 1968), which first appeared in 1964 and which marks the reappearance in psychoanalysis of the theory, even the notion, of seduction. When he explains deferred action in terms of the theory of primal fantasies, and primal fantasies in terms of scenes that were actually experienced in the course of phylogenesis, Freud inevitably introduces a fatal flaw into an otherwise innovatory notion.

To turn now to the topographical aspects of the theory – using the term in the wider sense of introducing the notions of internal and external into psychical conflict. Matters become dangerously confused here too. The notion of an internal attack, which was bound up with the idea of an internal foreign body, remains intact but *fantasy now replaces this ultimate psychical reality*. But if it is taken at face value, fantasy all too easily dissolved into the mists of the imaginary.

Once again, Freud cannot stop himself trying to reach the ground of a more objective reality; the origins of fantasy must inevitably be found in the drives, and the origins of the drives must lie in the biological. Although Freud argues that relations between representatives [*Reprasentanz*] provide a mediation between fantasy and the drives, the sequence is always the same: somatic excitation → drive → fantasy. Even the 'leaning' model is interpreted in this sense, even though it is intended to describe a process of emergence: the drive from within is likened to a transition from soma to psyche, and the soma−psyche opposition is open to all the obvious criticisms. But at the height of the seduction theory (Freud, 1985, p. 239) a very different causal sequence is established. Here, the sequence goes from depth to actuality: memories of scenes give rise to 'impulses' [*Impulse*] which are in terms of the development of Freud's thought, the true forerunners of the drives. Both a direct and an indirect path are outlined, with the latter making a transit through inter-mediary of fantasies as shown in figure 3.1.

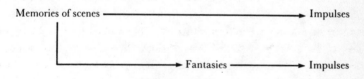

Memories of scenes ⟶ Impulses

Fantasies ⟶ Impulses

Figure 3.1

The third aspect of the theory, namely the language and translation model outlined in the letter of 6 December, disappears almost completely. Remants of it, or rather a new version of it, are to be found in Ferenczi (1933); it seems obvious that Ferenczi's article on the confusion of tongues, to which I have often referred, cannot really be chronologically related to Freud's writings in that Ferenczi certainly had no knowledge of the letter to Fliess, which was hidden away in the bottom of a trunk and which had, so everyone believed, been lost. But it can be seen as a sort of preface to the

general theory of seduction, and we can therefore defy chronology by claiming that it belongs to what I will call 'the post-
1964 period'.

Progress at the level of factuality: precocious seduction

Whilst the seduction theory undergoes a sort of repression
and dismemberment in Freud's writings, and whilst that
process could be described in greater detail, we will now
return to the 'factuality' column in table 3.1 in order to stress
that here, on the contrary, Freud makes considerable progress
in analysing the facts. Freud takes an important step when
he introduces a second level; the level of what I am calling
precocious seduction. The perverse father, who was the major
figure in infantile seduction, now makes way for the *mother*,
especially in the *pre-oedipal* relationship. Throughout this
period, Freud repeatedly returns to this theme. Every time
he reassesses his views on seduction, he adds that, ultimately,
its centre of gravity, and in a sense its truth, is to be found in
precocious seduction by the mother. This is his way of
indicating that he has not simply abandoned the idea of
seduction and, moreover, that he has refined it. Freud is now
concerned with essentials, and not with anecdotal scenes *à la*
Nabokov. To cite the later canonical passages from the *New
Introductory Lectures*, where Freud (1933, p. 120) decribes the
pre-Oedipus pre-history of girls: 'Here, however, the fantasy
touches the ground of reality [*den Boden der Wirklichkeit*] for it
really was the mother who by her activities over the child's
bodily hygiene inevitably stimulated [*erwecken musste*], and
perhaps even aroused for the first time, pleasurable sensations
in her genitals.' This is a vital step forward; it takes us back
in time, as it refers to the very first months of life, but it also
takes us further back in terms of the category of reality, and
it is there that the facts of seduction have to be located. Here
we are not exactly dealing with *realität*, a term which designates reality in the sense of 'real events' but with *Wirklichkeit*
(efficacy, effective reality), and that category take us beyond

contingency and peripeteia. The same could be said of the term *musste*. It is *inevitable* that the mother should arouse pleasurable sensations; that possibility is inscribed in the situation and does not depend upon contingent factors. On the other hand, Freud does sin by omission in that he fails to bring out the importance of this second level of seduction. He fails to analyse its universality and inevitability, even though they mean that it is a basic human given. He fails to extend precocious seduction to sexuality in general, limits its effects to the arousal of sensations in the genitals, and fails to note that arousal also occurs at the level of the erogeneity of the whole body, and especially at the level of oral and anal erogeneity. He fails to make allowance for the mother's unconscious, as he does throughout his work, except on rare occasions. Finally, and more seriously still, he fails to locate precocious seduction within the body of theory which would have given it its full value, had it not been destroyed. The convenient distinction we have been making between the line of factuality and that of theory is in fact an artificial distinction; we cannot develop a *general theory of seduction* unless we can arrive at a precise definition of what we can now call *primal seduction*; conversely, Freud's attempted reassessment of the phenomenon of seduction was doomed to failure because his work was grounded in a theory which combined a biologistic theory of the drives with an anthropo-phylogenetic theory of fantasy.

3.5 Towards the general theory of seducton

No return to infantile seduction

We now come to the contemporary period, to the post-1964—7 period, but I have no intention of jumping on the bandwagon of exploring Freud's prehistory and stressing his early interest in psychopathological or even forensic studies of the sexual abuse of children. The remarkable thing about a book like Masson's *Suppression of the Seduction Theory* (Masson, 1984) is that the title is completely at odds with the text, which has absolutely nothing to say about Freud's seduction *theory*. Almost all contemporary texts which refer to the 'seduction theory' (Balmary, 1979; Malcolm, 1984; Krüll, 1986) rely at best upon the rather vague notion that, for a while, Freud attributed great importance to seduction as a factor in . . . the aetiology of the neuroses. The authors appear to have no understanding of the extremely complex workings of the theory itself. Masson's chapter on 'Freud at the Paris Morgue' stresses the interest Freud took in the sexual abuse of children; it is not without a certain historical interest, but it represents an unthinking return to infantile seduction; the claim that Freud was afraid to go any further and the suggestion that we should go back to something on which he may have *dwelled too long*, namely obvious sexual abuse, means, in my view, falling back upon a crude opposition between reality and fantasy, the whole point of the theory being that it allows us to go beyond that opposition.

The activity—passivity pair re-examined

The generalization I am proposing therefore implies that we have to begin by raising certain theoretical questions. Indeed, its first foundations are highly philosophical, and take the form of a re-examination of the 'activity—passivity' pair. It is greatly to Freud's credit that he traces both the origins of the theory of drives and, in chronological terms, the beginnings of sexual life back to this pair; that he does so is in itself a tribute to his courage (cf. the article on 'Activity—Passivity' in Laplanche and Pontalis, 1973). In a sense he therefore contradicts in advance what is now the most 'modern' description of relations between adults and children: interaction. If we did restrict ourselves to a purely behavioural description of relations between two living individuals, regardless of whether or not they belong to the same generation (or even species), it would be a very shrewd observer who could tell the difference between activity and passivity. As Freud (1915a, p. 122) puts it: 'Every instinct is a piece of activity; if we speak loosely of passive instincts, we can only mean instincts whose *aim* is passive.' But even when he refers to the aim of the instinct, Freud gets into a muddle, as we can see from the very simple example of the initial situation of breast-feeding. In the *New Introductory Lectures*, Freud (1933, p. 115) asserts that 'A mother is active in every sense towards her child', whereas in 'Leonardo' (in other respects a very coherent text) he seems disconcerted by the fact that Leonardo recalls that, as a child, he passively took the tail of the vulture between his lips (Freud, 1910a). Freud, on the other hand, sees oral erotism or sucking at the breast as an action on the part of the infant (cf. Laplanche 1986, 1981, pp. 82−7). Matters are, then, somewhat confused and, unless we can distinguish between active and passive on the basis of strict criteria, the confusion plays into the hands of the interactionists. If we wish to make a distinction between the two, we should not, then, be afraid to appeal to the philosophers, and especially the Cartesians, who raised the question of activity−passivity in intersubjective relations in particularly acute terms by referring both to mutual relations between created things and to relations between created things and God.

The Cartesians

We can refer here to either Descartes, Spinoza or Leibniz. When Descartes examines the relationship between cause and effect, he argues that there must be 'at least as much reality' in the cause as in the effect (a thesis which provides the basis for one of his arguments to prove the existence of God). Spinoza (1677) goes even further by relating passivity to an inability to control something that takes place within us.[21] Leibniz (1714, §49, 50) is even clearer on this point:

A created thing is said to act outwardly in so far as it has perfection, and to be acted upon by another in so far as it is imperfect [appearances to the contrary notwithstanding, this theological notion of perfection is not to be understood in any absolute sense; there are different degrees of perfection]... One created thing is more perfect than another when we find in the first that which gives an *a priori* reason for what occurs in the second. This is why we say that one acts upon the other.

With Ferenczi

By using the strict criterion of 'more' (more content, more signification and therefore more message) we can now approach the child's primal situation in an attempt to define it over and beyond all its variations. Here, we can look for support to Ferenczi (1933), whose daring allows us to get away from the exclusive 'familialism' which weighs so heavily upon all psychoanalytic thought. The fact that a child is brought up by *parents*, or even by *its* parents, is, ultimately, a *contingency*, even if it is rooted in biology and human history, and not a universal fact which is necessary in itself. The primal situation outlined by Ferenczi describes a child's encounter with the adult world. *Ultimately*, and whatever distortions may result from the fact, it is possible to become a human being without having a family; it is not possible to do so without encountering an adult world. It should be noted in passing that a rereading of Margaret Mead's writings on comparative anthropology might perhaps lead us to the same conclusion; she postulates that, over and beyond cultural variations, the universal fact is the problem of how the newborn child gains access to the adult world.

However, the adult world is not an objective world which the child has to discover and learn about in the same way that it learns to walk or to manipulate objects. It is characterized by the existence of messages (defined in the broadest sense; they may be linguistic mesages, or simply language-based messages, and can be either prelinguistic or paralinguistic) which ask the child questions it cannot yet understand.

The child has to make sense of them and give an answer, which amounts to the same thing.

I agree with Ferenczi up to a point, but only up to a point, as the expression 'confusion of tongues' does not appear to me to be quite adequate. There are indeed such things as adult *languages*; they include verbal language, the language of gestures, the language of conventions, sign langage, and the language of affects. The child has the potential to enter into these languages; its potential to do so is at once natural, instrumental and affective. But, I stress, the problem is not simply one of acquiring one or more of these 'languages', or of comparing two different languages and their respective logics and signifying batteries. We know perfectly well that it is quite possible to acquire languages or to establish a correspondence between languages without using a grammar or a dictionary, and without leaving anything out.

To adapt a science-fiction image suggested by Freud (1908, pp. 211-12), it is tempting to think of how an extra-terrestrial might react to our civilization or, more simply, of the reserved welcome Pizarro received from the Incas. The latter example teaches us that, whatever differences there may be at the level of mental structures, history or even referents, the confusion of tongues always finally gives way to some ordered modality of correspondence and acquisition. To go back to the child; it finds its own way in to a pre-existing language, and has no need of a teacher. A child inhabits language.

An unknown meaning

It is at this precise point, therefore, that we have to go far beyond Ferenczi, but that does not mean that we have to take the Lacanian path. Ferenczi stops short of the further consideration that what he calls the 'language of passion' (adult language) is traumatic only in so far as it conveys an unknown meaning, or only in so far as it manifests the presence of the parental unconscious. But, and it is here that

I disagree with Lacan, that manifestation of the unconscious is irreducible to the polysemic potentialities of language in general: the problem is, as I see it, still that of the individual unconscious.

In an attempt to bring all these elements together, we can say that that the encounter between adult and child entails an essential relationship between activity and passivity which is bound up with the inescapable fact that the psyche of the parent is 'richer' than that of the child. But, unlike the Cartesians, we cannot speak of a greater 'perfection' in this context as the adult's strength is also a source of weakness: the adult is divorced from his unconscious.

Enigmatic signifiers

I am, then, using the term *primal seduction* to describe a fundamental situation in which an adult profers to a child verbal, non-verbal and even behavioural signifiers which are pregnant with unconscious sexual significations. We do not have to look far to find concrete examples of what I call *enigmatic signifiers*. Can analytic theory afford to go ignoring the extent to which women unconsciously and sexually cathect the breast, which appears to be a natural organ for lactation? It is inconceivable that the infant does not notice this sexual cathexis, which might be said to be perverse in the sense that that term is defined in the *Three Essays*. It is impossible to imagine that the infant does not suspect that this cathexis is the source of a nagging question: what does the breast want from me, apart from wanting to suckle me, and, come to that why does it want to suckle me?

In any discussion of enigmatic signifiers, pride of place must, however, be given to what is known as the primal scene. Inevitably, I refer to the original text, to the first text in which Freud (1900, p. 585) describes how the child perceives parental coitus:

It is, I may say, a matter of daily experience that sexual intercourse between adults strikes any child who may observe it as something uncanny [*unheimlich*] and that it arouses anxiety in them. I have explained this anxiety by arguing that what we are dealing with is a sexual excitation with which their understanding is unable to cope and which they also, no doubt, repudiate [we will be speaking of 'repression' later; here, 'repudiation' is used in much the same sense] because their parents are involved in it, and which is therefore transformed into anxiety and [here we find the inescapable 'first' theory of how sexual excitation is transformed into anxiety].

The enigma: the mechanism behind primal seduction

What I want to underline in this passage, which anticipates the idea of primal seduction, is that there is something about this scene that only the work of understanding can master, something which is traumatic and which is therefore repressed, precisely because it has not been tamed.

If, like Freud in his later writings, we attempt to include seduction within the catch-all category of primal fantasy, and put it on a par with the scene in which a child observes its parents having sexual intercourse, we will fail to notice that the relationship between the two is hierarchical, that it is not a relationship of equivalence or juxtaposition. For the child, the so-called 'primal scene' *is* a seduction, a primal seduction. The sight of its parents having intercourse allows, or forces, the child to see images and fragments of traumatic scenarios which it cannot assimilate because they are to a certain extent opaque to the actors themselves. Melanie Klein's later notion of a 'combined parent-figure' clearly illustrates this aspect: the parents are joined in an eternal act of coitus which combines orgasm [*jouissance*] with death, whilst the baby is denied the ability to take part and *therefore* to symbolize.

The two great enigmas which Freud identifies as mobilizing the child's 'theoretical' activity, and as resulting in the 'sexual theories of children' (Freud, 1908) belong to the same register: the arrival of a new baby and gender difference.

Once again, it is the adults' own inability to explain these enigmas which produces the traumatic effect.

It will be obvious that I regard 'primal seduction' as including situations and forms of communication which have nothing to do with 'sexual assault'. The *enigma* is in itself a *seduction* and its mechanisms are unconscious. It was not for nothing that the Sphinx appeared outside the gates of Thebes before Oedipus's drama began.

Relations between three levels of seduction

Not the least of Leonardo da Vinci's merits is that he (and Freud's 'Leonardo') shows us the three levels of seduction we have been discussing: paedophile seduction (homosexual in his case), precocious seduction by the mother and, finally, primal seduction, as represented by the unforgettably *enigmatic* smile of the Mona Lisa, the Virgin and St John. We must, that is, remember that primal seduction does not take away the importance of the other two levels; on the contrary, it provides them with their foundations. Nor can primal seduction be considered the first stage in a deferred-action model, with precocious or infantile seduction as a second stage. Primal seduction is the ultimate essence of the other two stages, and it alone introduces the 'activity—passivity' disymmetry. The 'attentions of a mother' or the 'aggression of a father' are seductive only because they are not transparent. They are seductive because they are opaque, because they convey some thing enigmatic.

Precocious seduction, for its part, deserves our full attention if we are to construct a new theory of drives. That theory centres on the notions of erotogenic zones, of the somatic source of the drives, and of anal, oral or phallic component drives. But if we are to escape the impasse of a speculative psychology — and even in Freud's day, psychoanalysis found itself in an impasse when it began to ask what the sexual process might mean at the level of a non-genital erotogenic zone — it must be recalled that the erotogenic zones are transit areas and sites of exchange. They are primarily and primordially a focus for the attentions of the mother. The conscious motivation behind the concern she shows for her child's bodily hygiene is solicitude, but unconscious wishful fantasies are also at work. And finally, it is only by looking at primal and precocious seduction that we can bring out the true importance of the facts of infantile seduction, that we can release them from the theoretical ghetto to which they have been confined for so long.

Let me point out once more that the 'infantile seduction, precocious seduction, primal seduction' sequence does not take us from the real to the mythical, as we have to reject the use of the term 'mythical' (or 'mythical time') on the grounds that it is an attempt to deny the existence of the primal: the primal gives a more profound meaning to the notion of real (by which I obviously mean the human real) because it takes us closer to the situations which found the real: the primal is a category of effectivity, of *Wirklichkeit*.

The general theory of seduction

The seduction theory, in its general form (the right-hand column in table 3.1), must be reconstructed on the basis of a specific conception of a hierarchy of *seductions*. This reconstruction will allow us to move from Freud's 'special' theory to a new level, in precisely the same way that physics made the transition from the special theory of relativity to the general theory. The general theory is no longer restricted to pathology, which was an essential feature of Freud's thinking in the pre-1897 period; it is intended to found the structure of the psychical or soul apparatus in general; and it invalidates the appeal to biology and phylogenesis, though it may justify it at a later stage. The theory must be able to use the mechanism of repression to account for the constitution and continued existence of an unconscious, and for the 'drive' effect that is inevitably associated with it. But the model must also be able to take in 'treatment', and its effects and limitations.

I have already outlined a general but extremely detailed schema in the context of a discussion of the drives (Laplanche, 1985). It represents an encounter between an individual whose psycho-somatic structures are situated predominantly at the level of need, and signifiers emanating from an adult. Those signifiers pertain to the satisfaction of the child's needs, but they also convey the purely interrogative potential of other messages — and those other messages are sexual. These enigmatic messages set the child a difficult, or even impossible, task of mastery and symbolization and the attempt to perform it inevitably leaves behind unconscious residues. These are what Freud (1985, p. 208) terms *fueros* [literally the ancient privileges enjoyed by certain regions under Spanish law; tr.]; I refer to them as the source-objects of the drives. We are not, then, dealing with some vague confusion of tongues, as Ferenczi would have it, but with a highly specific inadequacy of languages. The language of the child is not adequate to that of the adult. What is more important, the language of the adult is not adequate to the source-object that acts upon him.

The centrality of the 'translation' viewpoint

If we now return to the three viewpoints we identified in Freud's first theory, namely the temporal, topographical and 'translation' viewpoints, we can now see that the temporal viewpoint can only be understood on the basis of the translation and semiological viewpoint, as it is only within the domain of translation and secondary elaboration that the meaning of the curious effect known as 'deferred action' becomes comprehensible. The diagram given in the letter of 6 December 1896 (Freud, 1985, p. 310) still has a certain programmatic value, but it will be recalled that initially the column marking the first *Wz* (*Wahrenumngszeichen*: 'indication of peception') remains enigmatically blank, and that no one has commented on the fact. And how, in all honesty, could perception alone supply *indications*? If it were simply a matter of the perception of inanimate objects, perception would at best supply an index. If it were simply a matter of indications, of purely factual traces or of residues devoid of all semiological *intentionality* how could they suggest *even an initial translation* to the subject ? We can therefore state that the first indication of perception, or the first inscription in the psychical apparatus is the enigmatic signifier, and that it is inscribed before any attempt is made to translate it. And if we bear Freud's theorization in mind, this obviously implies that what he calls the 'experience of satisfaction' has to be called into question.

Modalities of metabola

The human being is, and will go on being, a self-translating and self-theorizing being. Primal repression is merely the first founding moment in a life-long process. I have outlined a schema to illustrate this process: the schema for the substitution of signifiers or for the various modalities of metabola (of. in particular Laplanche, 1981). The schema reproduced below is in part derived from Lacan, but it also differs from his schemata and has in fact been criticized by him. It illustrates how one signifier—signified pair is subjected to the metabolizing action of a pair of signifiers (the term 'metabolizing' is explained below).

$$\frac{S1}{s} \times \frac{S2}{S1}$$

This looks like a mathematical formula and it can in a sense be treated mathematically, but we are not dealing with higher mathematics or topology. To begin at the left: the signified (s) may be either an accessible signifier or a more inaccessible signifier; in the case of the first parental signifiers, s

is simply replaced by a question mark ('What does he/she/it want with me?'). Turning now to the right-hand member of the formula, we have to examine the relationship between S2 and S1. That relationship may be *one of similarity* or *one of contiguity*. Unlike the Lacanians, the post-Lacanians and even my friend Rosolato, I believe that substitution can pivot on signifiers which are bound together by contiguity *or* on signifiers which are bound together by similarity. When the link between S1 and S2 is (primarily) one of analogy, the metabola is said to be a metaphor; when the link between S1 and S2 is one of pure contiguity, the metabola is said to be a metonymy. Metabola is therefore a genre common to both metaphor and metonymy; the link between any two signifiers is in fact usually *both* one of contiguity *and* one of similarity. Metaphor and metonymy are abstractions and are rarely found in a pure state. We usually have a combination of the two.

What is the outcome of the operation of 'multiplication' or metabolization? In mathematical terms, it is possible to imagine two possible outcomes. The first is 'simplification'; if S1 simply disappears, the result will be S2. To use non-mathematical terminology, a new signifier is substituted for the old and nothing remains of it at the level of the signified. This is what I call an 'amnesiac' substitution in that it abolishes the old signifier. Take the example of etymological metabolization. With the passage of time, one signifier replaces another: S1 was once a Greek or Sanskrit signifier, but no one now knows, *even unconsciously*, what it was. The other schema is, in algebraic terms, a pure contrivance, but it is still suggestive; both the 'S1's in the original formula remain, but they now appear below the bar:

$$\frac{S2}{\underline{s}}$$
$$\frac{S1}{S1}$$

In mathematical terms, the formula is absurd because the old signifier is now its own denominator. We will adopt this schema as the pattern for the repressive metabola which results in the formation of the drive's source-object.

All this is in fact very schematic, as we are still dealing with elements of two kinds of result: part — but only part — of S1 is wrested out of its obscurity, and part of it is repressed. On the other hand, we must also make allowance for what is known as symbolization; this occurs when different types of metabola combining metonymy and metaphor are interwoven. It is this tissue, this symbolizing net, which gradually allows us to wrest something of the primal repressed from its obscurity.

The topography of the ego and the temporality of repression: a new view

Let me now say a few words as to how the topographical viewpoint is to be integrated into the general theory of seduction. The topography outlined by Freud in his so-called second theory (id, ego, super-ego) marks a vast improvement on his first model. But it would be a mistake to believe that the topography is therefore unaffected by the problem of its own genesis, or by the essential role played by *repression* in establishing the agencies. The topographical viewpoint is essential if we are to understand repression, but repression is indispensable to any understanding of the topographical viewpoint. There are, I would say, different levels of repression and different levels of topographical evolution. The levels of repression are already marked by the distinction between primal repression and secondary repression, or repression in the true sense. I insist, to begin with, on the fact that these levels of repression do not necessarily correspond to the hierarchy of primal seduction, precocious seduction and infantile seduction. That hierarchy is not a temporal sequence, and primal seduction is a support for, or the motor behind,

precocious seduction, infantile seduction, adult seduction and
even analytic seduction.

The point that has to be made here is that the two moments
of primal repression are indissociable from the movement
which results in the creation of the ego. Initially, there is no
'ego'. Alternatively, if we do wish to use the term 'ego' in
connection with this early stage, we can say that it coincides
with the whole individual or, to be more accurate, with the
periphery that delineates the individual. At this stage, we
have a body-ego, as Freud puts it. The second stage of
primal repression concerns the nascent ego-as-agency; the
ego-agency is now *part* of the apparatus, and it is made in the
image of the whole. It is therefore a metaphor for the biological
whole, but it is also an organ for the whole, and it exists
within a metonymic contiguity with the whole. Figure 3.2
indicates that the relationship between the different levels of
the ego is not simply one of parallelism or inclusion; it is
based upon tangents. It clearly shows why Leonardo da
Vinci could say that the windows of the body are the 'windows
of the soul'; but they are also the windows of the ego.

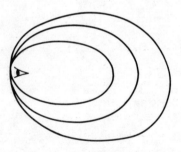

Figure 3.2

The stage (or repeated *stages*) of the appearance of the ego
— and it should not been seen as a unique period which is
cut off from everything else or which is self-contained — has
to be described as a period of *primary narcissism*, in the basic
sense in which Freud defines that term in his inaugural

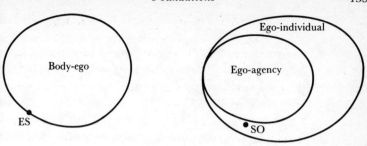

Figure 3.3

paper 'On Narcissism: An Introduction' (1914).[22] In figure 3.3, the position of the enigmatic signifier (ES) differs from one configuration to the next, depending on whether the ego does or does not exist as an agency. Initially, the enigmatic signifier is external, or, so to speak, embedded in the periphery of the ego. To put it in more concrete terms, it is implanted in the periphery of the individual, and primarily in the points known as erotogenic zones. In the second stage the enigmatic signifier or, to be more precise, its repressed residue, or the source-object (so), becomes internal; it is still external to the ego or embedded in its periphery but, given that the ego is more restricted than the individual (who can be represented in truly spatial terms), it is an internal—external element which, as far as the ego is concerned, acts from the outside.

These levels of binding and synthesis, the way in which the envelopes of the ego envelope one another, and these tangents or multitangents are, as I have argued more than once (Laplanche, 1980a, pp. 182–210; 1980c, pp. 237–47), the very things that allow us to understand both the ambiguities and the productivity of a model such as that of the vesicle in *Beyond the Pleasure Principle* (see figure 3.4).

A model of this kind is not, however, static; envelopes can both contract and dilate. Certain of them may eventually

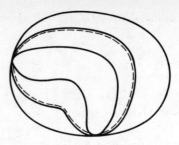

Figure 3.4

coincide anew, one of the best examples being the way in which the envelope of a dream can coincide with the somatic envelope of the dreamer. Others may be destroyed or become extremely dilated, and I think that it would be quite appropriate to pick up the theory of the ego at the very point where it was abandoned, only to be fundamentally distorted by what is known as 'ego psychology'. The work of Paul Federn (Federn, 1952) would provide an excellent starting point in both historical and theoretical terms.

What type of reality is the reality of 'primal represson'? It is no more a mythical time than is 'repression in the true sense' (as has sometimes been suggested), but nor is it directly accessible to punctual observation. The explanation for this is very simple, and it is in no sense a metaphysical explanation: primal repression is governed by the logic of deferred action, and it is a two-stage process. It can be identified or inserted into a chronology, but it can never be situated at a specific point in time, as is very clear from a book like Silvia Bleichmar's study (1985) of clinical child psychoanalysis.

Deferred action, which comes into play between the two stages of primal repression, also intervenes in primal repression itself. In concrete terms, this implies that primal repression has to be sealed if it is to be maintained: *secondary repression is needed*. And it is at this precise point that we find a place for the Oedipus, the castration complex and the formation of the super-ego.

The super-ego: a non-metabolizable imperative?

Given that we are now outlining a possible reworking of Freud's topography, I would like to say a few words about the super-ego. It is well known that a schematic opposition is drawn between the early instinctual super-ego, which was essentially Melanie Klein's discovery, and the later super-ego. The latter is made up of cultural imperatives and is signified by commandments; Freud tells us that it is bound up with the law. The general theory of seduction means, however, that this opposition loses much of its pertinence. If, that is, the drive originates in messages (but not, of course, solely in verbal messages), we have to conclude that there is no initial or natural opposition between the instinctual and the intersubjective, or between the instinctual and the cultural. The general theory of seduction centres upon the notion of an enigma, and it may therefore help us to elaborate a theory of the super-ego and of its imperatives. Our other guide is a philosophical reflection on this topic, and that reflection centres upon (but does not conclude with) Kant's analysis of the notion of the imperative (Kant, 1785). I merely wish to point out that, for Kant, all previous theories of morality had been founded on the conception of heteronomy; they were, that is, not centred on the subject, but were eccentric to the subject adcentred on relations with God, the species or the idea of the Good. The imperative that governed those ethics, and the law that stemmed from them, is referred to as being hypothetical or deducible from something else. The hypothetical imperative states: 'If you want that, do this.' If you want to please God and to ensure your salvation, if you want to conform to the idea of the Good, if you want society to function properly...then you must behave in this way'. In Kant's view, the hypothetical imperative therefore belongs to the realm of rules of skill, of technical rules, of the best possible adaptation of means to ends via the intermediary of 'if': the best way to ensure your salvation is, to take the example of Freud's great imperatives, not to kill your father and not to sleep with your mother.

Kant contrasts the hypothetical imperative with what he calls the categorical imperative on the grounds that the latter contains no *if* clause. It states 'You must do this, full stop.' If we look at it rather more closely, we find that Kant's categorical imperative is still in a sense hypothetical, even though it does involve a rather special kind of 'hypothesis', It states: 'If you wish to be free, you must act in such and such a fashion.' But unlike earlier imperatives, it involves, according to Kant, a purely formal deduction; in other works, specific imperatives can be deduced from the simple form of free will. The objection has quite rightly been raised that in reality no one has ever been able to deduce a single categorical imperative from this autonomy of the subject. It is precisely this kind of criticism that is addressed to Kant by certain modern critics and, implicitly, by Freud himself. I mention only three names of three thinkers who provide some interesting parallels: Levinas, in the field of the religious imperative, Lyotard and Freud. All three tell us that Kant's imperative is not as categorical as he claims it to be, because he himself deduces it (and, what is more, the deduction ends in failure); he makes the error of linking together the 'categorical' aspect and the 'autonomy' aspect. A true categorical imperative would not be autonomous, and it could not even be deduced from the notion of free will: it would be an implacable 'do this' which did not have to be justified at all. In the context of an extreme form of religion, namely the Judaic religion to which Levinas refers, God hands down the Law, and the Law does not have to be justified. Freud too raises the issue of the categorical aspect of moral imperatives by pointing out that the orders given by the super-ego are tyrannical and unjustifiable. Because of his mania for phylogenesis, Freud (1987, p. 15) traces this arbitrariness back to the first two tenets of the Father of the Horde: he was himself invulnerable and his possession of women must not be challenged (Freud uses *Satzungen* and not *Gesetze*, reading *Satzungen* and not *Setzungen*).

There are good grounds for looking very seriously into the notion that categorical imperative is born of the super-ego, and for dwelling on one specific aspect of it: categorical imperatives cannot be justified; they are certainly enigmatic in the same way that other adult messages are enigmatic; but not only are they unjustified, it is possible that they are unjustifiable, or in other words non-metabolizable. This means that they cannot be diluted, and cannot be replaced by anything else. They exist, and they are immutable and cannot be symbolized. They resist the schema for the substitution of signifiers.

I am simply putting forward a hypothesis, a suggestion for future discussion: are these imperatives totally non-metabolizable, defining metabole in the sense in which I used it earlier, or is it simply that they are non-metaphorizable? Is it possible that they are amenable to a certain metonymic derivation? Or, to put forward a further question for future and more detailed discussion, are the moral rules handed down by parents repressed, or are they impossible to repress and do they remain in the limbo of pre-repression to the extent that it is impossible to substitute something for them in an attempt to make do? And if categorical imperatives are, so to speak, trapped between the two stages of primal repression, should we not see them as psychotic enclaves inside the human pesonality as such?

At the end of this discussion of topography, we can only conclude that it is the whole of Freud's topography that has to be reworked and that we are not simply talking about the various labels that are pinned on to the 'agencies'. The term 'agency' in fact refers to a whole range of different realities: the id, the ego, the super-ego and the ideal agencies do not have the same nature or the same status; some are anthropomorphic and others are not; some are language-based, and others are not; some, like the ego, are specifically bound up with the problem of synthesis, and so on.

The theory of drives

How, then, are we to define our new theoretical task? How

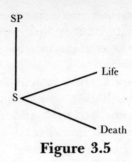

Figure 3.5

are we to resturcture the *theory of drives* within the framework
of the new foundations provided by general seduction? In my
view, we have to re-establish the distinctions introduced by
Freud, and give them a precise meaning.

As we know, we have to retain *both* theories of the drives,
and not merely one of them. The first theory contrasts self-
preservation with sexuality; the second, life drives with death
drives. We also have to recapture the ephemeral but vitally
important moment of their articulation in 'On Narcissism:
An Introduction'. We will therefore retain both these theoretical aspects, taking the view, once more, that moments in
the development of theory correspond to moments in the
development or genesis of the human subject. The schema is,
in other words, as shown is figure 3.5. We have already
looked at the workings of the self-preservation — sexuality
pair and we know that in Freud's more lucid moments it
corresponds, broadly speaking, to he opposition between drive
and instinct or, to use what I regard as a preferable terminology, between drive and function (function, being characterized by patterns which may be instinctive, is closer to self-
preservation). The critical exposition devoted to these terms
in chapter 2 indicates that I am not neglecting the level of
self-preservation, its importance, its failings or, of course, the
interest of the scientific explorations it has stimulated and
continues to stimulate. But we have also noted that it is the
reduction of the sexual level to self-preservation — and this is

a *real* human phenomenon — which produces the theoretical reduction we are criticising. Whilst self-preservation does have a role to play, it must be quite categorically stated that it not a protagonist in psychical conflict. We do not renounce sexuality for fear of losing our lives, but we do renounce it for other reasons; for example, for fear of not being loved. Self-preservation may be the battlefield, and it may be a victim in the sense that functions can be adversely affected by a conflict which does not take place at their level. There are countless examples, and those given by Freud are telling; in, for instance, 'The Psychoanalytic View of Psychogenic Disturbance of Vision' (Freud, 1910b), he shows that psychical conflict can have its effects at the level of vision (hysterical blindness). This does not, however, mean that the function of vision, as defined by its self-preservative finality, is involved in the conflict. One also thinks of 'Inhibitions, Symptoms and Anxiety' (Freud, 1926a), where Freud reveals the sexual meaning of the inhibition of certain functions, walking and writing being prime examples.

Is it necessary to retain the term *pulsion*, which was coined to translate Freud's *Trieb* (from *Trieben*, 'to push'). The answer is far from obvious. If we do retain it, we must at least divorce it from the biological. The human sexual drive is not initially biological, even if it does become biological at the later stage of genitality. In my view, it is, none the less, useful to retain the drive problematic as it answers four needs and meets four requirements of the psychoanalytic experience.

The case for drives: four requirements of psychoanalytic experience

The first requirement is that of *causality*. I am not necessarily talking about determinism; the notion of the drive accounts for the fact that we are not our own cause, but that we are indeed 'driven' or 'pushed' [*getrieben*]. It might even be said that the theory of drives is the last refuge of causality, which has been completely banished elsewhere; in contemporary scientific thought it was been rejected in favour of other notions such as that of legality, statistical or otherwise. The drive may therefore be the last real refuge of the notion of cause, its homeland and its home territory. No doubt that is what Lacan is getting at with his puns on *cause* and *chose* ('cause' and 'thing').

The second reason for retaining the notion of the drive is that it is inextricably bound up with the notion of the psychical representative. But at this point our 'new foundations' add a new urgency to this requirement. A drive is not, as Freud suggests all too often, some unknown form of energy which inexplicably attaches itself to representatives. The drive is in fact the force behind representatives which have acquired a separate status of their own: the status of the repressed and of the primordial unconscious.

There is a third sense in which Freud's notion of the drive is still useful; it describes the binding of component instincts to *determinate zones in the body*, and all that it implies, namely the notion of 'stages' or, rather, of types of organization corresponding to those zones of the body and to their workings. As we know, the seduction theory provides a different basis for the notion of erotogenic zones, in that it introduces the idea of 'precocious seduction'.

Lastly, the fourth sense in which Freud's realism is still relevant is that it enables us to account for phenomena which are bread and butter for a psychoanalyst: displacement, reversal into the opposite, separation of affect and idea, transformation into anxiety and so on. A theory which pays due attention to representatives and especially to the inscription of enigmatic signifiers is in a much better position to account for such phenomena, which have to be described as metabolizations, than any biologistic theory.

Elements of the drive and the source-object

We will, then, retain the notion of the drive, but it has to be stripped of its 'mythical' characteristics. It is also probable that its *elements* will have to be rearranged. According to Freud's analysis, as exemplified by 'Instincts and their Vicissitudes' (1915a) in particular, there are four such elements: source, object, aim and pressure. According to the analysis we have made, the *source* can only be an unconscious residue of primal repression (Freud comes close to this view when he introduces thing-presentations). We will look later at the implications of applying the term 'object' to 'source'. But as I have already pointed out, it must also be stressed that a source is not purely representational, and that it is somatically anchored in the erotogenic zones as a result of the phenomenon of seduction. The notion of *aim* has to be retained in the sense that it refers to metaphorization, to the metaphoric action of the somatic processes of exchange; it is therefore bound up with the source and its somatic anchoring. Which leaves us with the question of *pressure*. Do we need this quantitative concept? Is it or is it not a constant force? If it is, as Freud states, a constant force, an unknown quantity in constant motion, why should we include it in our formula and what purpose does it serve? It does seem plausible that a given component drive might have a relatively constant force. I would argue, however, that its force is *relatively* constant and that this is true only for a determinate period of time. Using a physicalist terminology which does not necessarily have to be rejected, Freud (1915a, p. 122) defines the pressure of a drive as representing a 'demand for work'. But, and this is where our definitions diverge, that demand for work does not emanate directly from somatic sources, but from unconscious prototypes; to be more accurate, it emanates from the difference between those elements in the primal enigmatic signifiers which can be symbolized and those elements which cannot be symbolized. The constancy of this economic factor is, then, relative, and one of the features of the analytic process is that the processes of symbolization weaken its compulsive power. It also seems that the repetition of the process of seduction may give a new stimulus to the drives. If, in short, we wish to retain the notion of instinctual energy at all cost, we have to accept the idea that it is only relatively constant, and that psychical processes can both increase and decrease its pressure.

Seduction as the truth behind Anlehnung [leaning on]: a note

Before going on to discuss the two types of drive and the subdivision of the sexual drive, let me say a word about the relationship between self-preservation and sexuality and make a comment on the notion of 'leaning on'. It is only because it has been rediscovered after having been seriously eclipsed that this notion has become so central to Freudian thought. Ever since Pontalis and I rediscovered it (see 'Anaclisis' in Laplanche and Pontalis 1973), it has been applied to anything and everything; for some time now, there has been talk of 'leaning on' in all possible contexts. The notion has been invoked in connection with the mother, the biological, the body. There is talk of 'leaning away from' and even of the body leaning on the soul. But, in Freud, there is no sense in which leaning on is an answer to a question relating to relations between body and soul. It refers to the way in which the sexual function is supported by the self-preservative function; *both can be said to be simultaneously psychical and somatic.* It is not that the sexual is 'more' psychical and that self-preservation is more 'somatic'; both are global aspects of a functioning which has a meaning.

So much for the way concepts have been distorted and debased since Freud's day. But even if we do use leaning on in its original — and proper — sense, it has to be remembered that *the theory of leaning emerges because of the vacuum created by the abandoning of the seduction theory in 1897.* Leaning is a valid notion in so far as it describes a certain mode of articulation, which we can represent by means of certain schemata (a dihedron, or the tub); it is not valid as a model of origins or genesis. We sometimes find in Freud the idea that the genesis of sexuality involves 'leaning', but if we take that idea seriously it must refer to the gradual emergence from within a biolog-

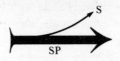

Figure 3.6

ical functioning of a divergency between self-preservation and sexuality. One possible schema is shown in figure 3.6.

This is in fact what Freud suggests in connection with the so-called 'sucking' model for oral sexuality. It may be possible to retain this schema, provided that we do not see it as a spontaneous or endogenous movement. We have here something resembling an onion with one layer of its skin peeled off, or a flower which has lost a petal. And, to make the point succinctly, onions do not peel themselves. Seduction peels what might be termed a sexual layer away from self-preservation. Seduction peels the onion of self-preservation; self-preservation does not split as a result of some indefinable endogenous movement.

Life drives and death drives

We will now look briefly at the field of the drive in the true sense of the word, or at what I term the second theory of drives: life and death drives. One point has to be hammered home from the outset: if categories such as the life and death of the biological subject, which derive from the concept of self-preservation, are to be applied outside the realm of self-preservation, they must obviously undergo a profound metabolization. 'Life and death in psychoanalysis' and 'life and death drives' do not refer to the life and death of a biological individual. But in a curious way, the drives do intertwine with the life and death that are ours in so far as we are individuals and in so far as it is our biological destiny to perpetuate our being until the moment of our death. *Both* the types of drives described by Freud *exist within the field of the sexual drive*. This is obviously true of Eros, but it is also true of the 'death drive'. It is impossible here to produce all the historical and theoretical evidence which allows us to state that the death drive is not a fundamentally new innovation, and that it is part of what Freud always calls 'sexuality' (of. Laplanche, 1981; 1986). The innovation of 1915—20 is not the death drive, but the life drive. In other words, sexuality is bound up with a whole object; I am referring to the sexuality which becomes love, meaning either love for the other or, in a fundamentally related sense, self-love or narcissism. It is the discovery of love for a whole object (the whole other, or the self as ego or whole object) that is new; and it is this discovery which forces Freud to correct the balance and to assert that the least narcissistic and least idyllic aspects of sexuality — its most destructive, fragmented and fragmenting aspects — are also present from the start. If we take a longitudinal section through Freud's thought and if we raise the question of what lies beneath the term 'death drive' (and after all we are under no obligation to retain a mere phrase, inspired or inspirational though it may well be), we find a restatement of the old thesis that sexuality is essentially conflictual and irreconcilably opposed to the ego. One of the many proofs of that is that, whilst he does postulate the existence of two kinds of drive, Freud never accepts that there might be two kinds of instinctual energy; he never accepts the existence of an energy specific to the death drive, of a *'destrudo'* (*destrudo* is not a Freudian term; there is no *destrudo*).

Drive and object

The life and death drives are both aspects of the sexual drive, and we have to succeed in defining them. In order to do that, we may have to turn to other writers for help, Klein being the obvious example. The so-called 'life' sexual drive corresponds to a *whole* and *totalizing* object; it is bound (in Freud's sense of continuing to exist in a more or less coherent manner, of not being fragmented) because it relates to a totalizing object or to an object than can be totalized. It seems to me that it is therefore more likely to undergo a metaphoric displacement rather than a metonymic displacement, for the very simple reason that only structures which display a certain totality and a certain internal articulation can lend themselves to the analogy which produces metaphoric substitution; analogies are only possible between units that display certain structurations and certain formal similarities at the level of their totality. The death drive, on the other hand, corresponds to a *part object* which is scarcely an object at all, as it is, even in Klein's description, unstable, shapeless and fragmented; it is, therefore, closer to metonymy than metaphor.

Drives, primary process, secondary process

A certain relationship can of course be established between these types of drive and the phenomena known as the primary and secondary processes; but we cannot establish a complete equation between the two, or say that the entire primary process is dominated by the death drive whilst the entire secondary process is dominated by the life drives. We have a complementary series rather than a real opposition, and that series runs through the entire psychical apparatus, from the deepest levels of the id, which is sworn to absolute fragmentation, to processes which are closely bound to the ego or the object, those being the processes revealed by narcissism. The absolute primary process and the absolute secondary process are linked by a series which distributes varying degrees of metaphor and metonymy, but there is no point at which we can speak of pure metonymy and pure metaphor.

The question of the source-object

Within the primary process itself, that is within unconscious processes, we find, then, a great diversity of functionings: a primary process in an almost pure state, or the functioning of

the death drive, and a primary process which is already
regulated to some extent, or the functioning of a life drive,
which is not specific to either the primary or the secondary
process. This means that the expression 'source object' may
be open to criticism on the grounds that it is simply inaccurate.
'Source' is fine, but what about 'object'? We can, I think, use
that term provided that we make a distinction between whole
and part objects, and concede that a part object is scarcely
an object at all, that it is closer to being an index rather than
a 'true' object. Indeed, I have sometimes made a distinction
between two types of drive: 'object drive' and 'index drive'.
But we also have to add that the *same* source-object is the
source of both, that it is the source of both the destructive
and the synthesizing aspects of the drive, depending on
whether it takes on a fragmented and part aspect or a whole
aspect.

All this seems to be very complicated at the theoretical
level, but it becomes even more complicated if we try to get
back to the level of psychical confilct. At a metapsychological
level, there is a clash of armies in the heavens, to use Freud's
image, and, in the last analysis, psychical conflict is a conflict
between life and death drives; to put it in more concrete
terms, day-to-day psychoanalytic experience reveals that it is
a conflict between binding and unbinding processes. This
does not mean that we have to promote binding, or that we
have to conclude that binding always works to the advantage
of biological life or even psychical life; extreme binding,
means extreme immobilization. In that sense, Lacan's
denunciations of the ego as an agency of fascination and
immobilization are, outrageous though they may be, still
valid. The psyche will certainly die if it disintegrates or
comes under the sway of the death drive, but it can also die if
it becomes too rigidly synthetic. The ego too can be a source
of death.

In the last analysis — and everything has to be restated in
much more concrete terms than this schema of the drives will
allow for — we should now have the basis for a description of

the nature of symbolization, and of how its history is pun-
ctuated by stages (I am not denying the existence of essential
stages such as the Oedipus and castration, even though I
would claim that they, as opposed to primal seduction, are
secondary stages); we should now be in a position to go
beyond the above suggestions, to work at a new theory of the
genesis and function of the agencies of the psyche and, of
course, to situate the various ways in which symbolization
may fail.

3.6   Afterword: the nature of the unconscious

In order to conclude this discussion of our theoretical
foundations and before going on to outline their practical
implications, I would like to look again at a polemic over the
nature of the unconscious which has been going on for decades.
In an early article, Leclaire and I (Laplanche and Leclaire,
1972) clearly outline the opposition, which is still pertinent,
between the realist view of the unconscious and the phenomenological view. The realist view, which is, broadly, Freud's
view, is what might be called a 'naïve' realism (the term is
not intended to have any pejorative connotations). It is based
primarily upon the experience of analytic treatment, of
psychical conflict or of symptoms, where it transpires that
whatever emerges from the unconscious intervenes as a reality
which comes into conflict with other realities. Both protagonists, the wish and the defence, exist at the same level of
reality and expression, and can even be intricated in compromise formations. Certain of the philosophical and ontological
arguments Freud uses to defend his realism are highly dubious,
debateable, or even self-contradictory. Referring to Kant, for
instance, he likens the unconscious to the 'thing in itself'; if,
argues Freud, we accept the existence of an unknowable
thing in itelf which lies beyond the realm of physical phenomena, why not adopt the same hypothesis with regard to the
psyche? In my view, this argument undermines the most

radical implications of the analytic discovery: if the unconscious is no longer a separate register, or if it is simply the unknowable backdrop to our whole psyche, recognition of its existence is simply a pious gesture which has no serious practical implications.

From phenomenology to realism

This 'realism of the unconscious' may be contrasted with what I call a phenomenological veiw of the unconscious, even though not all it proponents would describe themselves as phenomenologists. Its most talented exponents are Politzer (1928), Sartre (at his best) and, much more recently, Roy Schafer (1976). Very schematically, the phenomenological view is that the immanence of the unconscious is akin to the immanence of meaning within its various expressions. To take a simple example; for Politzer, a dream is a meaning which does not have to be realized, and which finds both a non-conventional expression in a dream and a conventional expression in the day-to-day language which is used to decode the dream. One mode of expression uses ordinary language; the other, an individual or invented language. There is no need to look for anything else, such as a third term or ultimate meaning. Meaning, even unconscious meaning, does not have to be realized.

I summarize these arguments in order to raise a question about our new foundations and, more specifically, about the general theory of seduction: does not this theory introduce a new and perhaps fundamental argument into the debate over the realism of the unconscious? To recapitulate: the primal situation we have described is an encounter between a child and an adult who proffers messages but does not grasp their full meaning. In describing the 'adult' protagonist, I was at pains to stress that there was, at that point, no need to adopt any hypothesis as to the nature of the unconscious; we simply had to accept that the unconscious was present in the sense that even its opponents accept its presence, in the sense that the 'phenomenologists' understand the term, or even in the sense in which we inevitably accept it in everyday life, as in the wonderful expression: 'You've just made a Freudian slip.' The primal situation described above has no need for the realism of the unconscious; its consequences will follow regardless. But the primal situation, primal seduction and the subsequent process of repression or primal metabolization will inevitably leave a residue. And that residue can only be something which has not been symbolized, or a designified signifier. In other words, whilst the realism of the unconscious is not an initial hypothesis which explains this process, it is the conclusion we have to reach. The realism of the unconscious is a clinical-theoretical deduction based upon a much more neutral initial description. We have only to accept Freud's discovery in a minimalist sense, or to accept that certain 'bungled actions' have a meaning of which the subject is unaware, without adopting any hypothesis as to the nature of this 'unawareness',- to reach the conclusion that the realist view of the unconscious alone is compatible with the workings of primal repression.

4

The Practical Task

It is, perhaps, a truism to stress that theory and practice are closely interwoven, that they are intimately dependent upon one another. But in the case of psychoanalysis, where the founding gesture is simultaneously practical and theoretical, their interdependence is of crucial importance. 'The Practical Task' is the title of Part II of *An Outline of Psychoanalysis* (Freud, 1938), the last work which Freud completed. But in that chapter Freud may perhaps give the impression that the relationship between theory and practice is one of application, which is why I suggest that we use expressions like 'putting to work' or 'putting to the test of practice'.

The crisis of 1897: theory and practice interwoven

Let us go back to the turning point of 1897 for a moment. In Freud's correspondence with Fliess we find consclusive evidence that theory and practice advance hand in hand. Practice is a living construct, and theory is immediately put to the test of practice. Failures, when they occur, are failures for both theory and practice. As we know, Freud was at this time working with a theory which was both 'special' and restrictive, and approached the unconscious from a purely psychopathological viewpoint. On the other hand, we have also seen that the theory inspired a practical hope: making the entire unconscious conscious. And that hope would have been quite legitimate, *were it true* that only neurotics and those suffering from mental illness had an unconscious. And did not Freud argue something very similar in connection with transference which, he thought, was a phenomenon found only in neurotics?

The need to revise the theory in 1897 was therefore experienced as a failure. In our terms it is indeed a failure in so far as the contradiction did not result in the transformation of the seduction theory. Failure may have been unavoidable, but the fact remains that the crisis also provides a positive model in that it affects both theory and practice.

Theory and practice divorced

There is nothing new about raising quesions about our actions and their limitations. But things have changed since 1897, and unfortunately we no longer ask the far-reaching questions that Freud asked. Practice and theory now go their separate ways. Theory is often disavowed or denigrated, largely as a result of English empirio-clinicalism. The imperialism of so-called clinicalism has now reached new heights; no text and no colloquium is immune to censorship unless it can produce a few scraps of case histories. It is forgotten that experience can inform theory, that theory is in itself a form of experience, that there is such a thing as theoretical practice. In a word, experience and empiricism have become confused.

How do things stand with practice? The greater part of the analytic world has lost its theoretical bearings. Because it has no lucid vision of its objectives and limitations, it all too often oscillates between despair and mad hopes. In the post-war Communist movement it was often said that nothing should be said that might discourage the Renault workers at Billancourt, meaning that the real nature of the Soviet regime had to be concealed at all cost. If we say that nothing should be said that might discourage the *treizième arondissement*, we begin to get some idea of the realities of French psychoanalysis. But who does most to sow despair? Those who point out that there are limits, or those who set off on impossible adventures in

areas where there are no limits? The headlong rush to
publish clinical material is one sign of this adventurism. I
give a clinical paper; you free-associate on the basis of my
paper; we hold a seminar on your free associations and so on.
What remains of the gradualism of psychoanalysis in all this?
There is, then, a crisis within practice. There is a crisis at the
level of principles: either there are no principles, or we fall
back upon the old cliches about dispelling illusions and
strengthening the ego, unless of course we opt for a substitute
mode of behaviour, constantly inject puns into analysis and
say that we are interpreting the signifier. Psychoanalysis is in
a state of crisis because it has no sense of where it is going
and because it has no vision of its dynamic, its indications,
its findings or its ends. And, finally, psychoanalysis is in a
state of crisis because of its practitioners; as we well know, in
the present climate anybody and everybody can set themselves
up as a psychoanalyst.

How will the new foundations I am proposing with the
general theory of seduction help to restore practice to its
rightful status? The question is too vast to be fully dealt with
here, and I will merely outline an answer in the form of three
points concerning, respectively, the analytic situation, transference and the process.

4.1   The situation

The 'setting': neither formalism nor a technical appliance

The *situation* means, as we know, a framework and rules. The
term *setting* is often used, but it tends to suggest something
which is purely arbitrary, or purely technical. The setting is
not a ritual. Nor is it a technical appliance; a psychoanalyst
does not set up a surgery in the way that a dentist does. And
nor is the setting an arbitrary law. It is all too easy to slip
from law to Law, which makes it possible to denounce minor
failures to comply with the Law as transgressions against a

so-called symbolic order. There is only a thin dividing line between law and formalism, and the terms lend themselves to facile inversions. Pure formalism is as meaningless as the unthinking rejection of form and there is no theoretical justification for either. When formalism loses its meaning it is tempting to say, 'To hell with it'. It is essential to adjust techniques to the needs of analysands and to introduce variations, but we have to be able to justify them. This reminds me of the sub-title Lacan (Lacan,1955, p. 323) chose for an article he was asked to produce on 'Les variantes de la cure type' ['Variations on the typical analysis']: '*Une question chauve-souris: l'examiner en plein jour*' ['A question for bats; examine it by daylight']. If we cannot let in at least some daylight, anything goes, Even the temporal and spatial limits of the situation are dissolved. To look rapidly at the issue of time limits as an analysis progresses, there is a gradual and un-thinking drift from 'psychotherapy' to 'psychoanalysis'. 'When am I going to put him/her on the couch?' 'Shall I ask him/her to lie on the couch for one session and then let him/her sit?' 'Should I ask him/her to sit in a rocking chair?' And conversely, as the end of the analysis approaches, we frequently hear patients asking: 'When will I get down to two sessions a week, doctor?' And then we have, 'When do I get down to one session?' Why not half a session? And so analysis becomes a sort of gradual therapy.

Psychoanalysis establishes something

In an attempt to break with this mood of self-doubt, let me hammer home two points and trace four guidelines. First of all, analysis establishes something: the terms 'contract' or 'pact', with their legalistic connotations, are quite inappropriate, unless we can recapture something of their primal meaning and speak of, say, a social 'contract' in the sense in which Rousseau uses that term. Psychoanalysis implies an inaugural gesture or set of gestures, and the arbitrary has to give way to the essential. And psychoanalysis always establishes something anew; right to the very end, to the final moment of the analysis. There is no gradual transition from analysis to outside the analysis.

The tub: a purely instinctual site

My second point is this: psychoanalysis establishes *a purely instinctual or sexual site*. Here theory comes to our help by making a clear distinction between self-preservation, or the field of interests, needs and adaptation, and the field of sexuality or libido. The analytic situation functions outside the realm of self-preservation and adaptational goals, but it exists on the basis of a complex schema. I have aleady outlined the 'tub' schema; it derives from the dream schema, or at least the schema described by Freud, but that does not mean that analysis is a dream in any sense. In sleep, the powers of movement and perception are paralysed, but the external field intervenes in analysis in a very different way. The whole point of the schema is that it provides a visual representation of the difference between the two. In dreams, the subject is denied both perception and expression through motricity. In analysis, there is no such break; the afferent 'arrows' continue to exist, but they are in a sort of tangential relationship to the circle representing the tub (see figure 4.1).

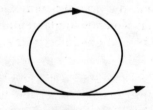

Figure 4.1

Adaptational interests are not, strictly speaking, excluded from what happens within the tub, although what hapens there is of the order of sexuality, love and hate (as we know, exclusion orders do not always have the desired effect!); they are made tangential. They are made tangential by the establishment of the spatio-temporal limits of the analysis, and above all by the analyst's refusals.

In using the term 'refusal' or 'refusing' I am attempting to bring out the implications of Freud's *Versagung* and we therefore have to describe the two major forms of analytic 'refusing'. At this point in the discussion, we are dealing with a *first form of refusing*, a refusal to work at the level of adaptation, to give advice, or to discuss means and ends. If, for example, a patient fails to turn up for a session, the analyst refuses to discuss his or her absence purely in terms of train times.

A site for primal seduction

My third point with regard to the situation is that it re-establishes a *site for primal seduction*. I am using the term precisely in the sense it was defined earlier: the seduction of the enigma. Precocious seduction and infantile seduction are obviously not enacted in psychoanalysis, unless its practice becomes perverted. It is *primal seduction alone* which comes into play here, and it does so in a much purer and more essential form than it does in childhood because, in childhood situations, it is always to some extent mediated by sexual gestures or sexual behaviour. This sheds a new light on the notion of the primal: the primal is not essentially that which comes first, but that which is fundamental; it is therefore not surprising that the primal should be at least potentially present in the early stages of life. But it is by no means impossible for a later situation such as analysis to reactivate the very *essence* of the primal. Here we have, I think, a possible point of articulation with Conrad Stein's (1986; 1987) conceptions and a basis on which to discuss his view that the primal means the present or the actuality of the analytic situation. On the other hand I strongly disagree with Stein when he claims that any relativism or 'subjectivism' which is centred on the analytic session (analytico-centrism, in the sense in which one can speak of ethnocentrism) reduces the infantile primal to the status of a myth which is forged a posteriori. In other words, it is still relevant to make, and to go on making, a distinction between deferred action (and the tension it implies between two or more psychical events) and retrospective fantasy (*Zurückfantasieren*) which, according to Jung himself, centres on the present moment, which is also its sole starting point. Dressing fantasy up as myth does nothing, in my view, to alter the basic problem: the efficacy of the infantile primal.

The situation establishes a primal relationship with the enigma and with its bearer who is, to borrow an expression used, if not elaborated upon, by Lacan, 'supposed to know' (Lacan, 1977, p. 230 ff.). This brings us to the essential element in the ethics of the psychoanalyst: counter-transference. There is talk of mastering counter-transference, using counter-transference, of counter-transference as affect, participation, implication, and so on. But perhaps that is missing the point, the point being that if the analyst must be in the position of one supposed to know, he must obviously refuse knowledge, but he must also refuse to let himself know. This refusal to know, this refusal of knowledge, is the second form of analytic 'refusing', the first being the refusal to adapt. This is the motor, the source of energy, and perhaps it is the source of a new energy, which propels the cure. The search for knowledge both enslaves and propels the analysand, just as it once propelled the small child.

Containing

My fourth and last point is this: the situation is a site for *containing* and holding. This is not my discovery; I have said so many harsh things about English 'empirio-clinicalism' that I must at least give Winnicott and Bion credit for the idea of a 'container'. To take up the tub schema again, I compare the holding environment to a cyclotron in which particles are accelerated by being bombarded with huge amounts of energy. A cyclotron which is not contained becomes an H-bomb. The major failing of Lacan and the Lacanians is perhaps their inability to grasp the notion of 'containing'. Regular sessions of standard length and a constant environment are important factors in containing, but its most important feature is the attention, or attentions, of the analyst. All analysts sometimes give in to the temptation to open a letter or to answer the telephone, but a systematic lack of attention destroys the essential element of holding: limits disappear, and the session is dissolved. And the presence of limits is all the more necessary in that we encourage or induce an unbinding discourse.

4.2 Transference

The situation is a transference

Having dealt with the four cardinal points of the *situation*, we can now turn to *transference*. But we immediately have to qualify the distinction we have just introduced by adding that the situation is in itself a transference. Psychoanalytic thinking about transference is making gradual progress. Although far from recent, Daniel Lagache's report (Lagache, 1950) sums up the situation well: progress has been made in that transference is no longer seen as a symptom produced by neurotics or even as a symptom for which the analysand is responsible; as Lagache and Ida MacAlpine (MacAlpine 1950) put it, analysis 'produces' or 'induces' transference in a very real sense. We now have to go further still, look beyond the term 'production' and state that it is because *it is in itself a transference* that the situation can re-establish a primal situation.

At this point, it becomes necessary to criticize universally accepted conceptions which, despite some variation in their content, are based upon Freud's own statements. Freud tells us that transference means the reproduction of stereotypes which are archaic, dated and ill-adapted to the present situation. Analytic neutrality encourages transference to such a degree that the various pathological mechanisms found in a neurosis become concentrated into what is known as a transference neurosis. During the course of the analysis, neurotic patterns of behaviour are exemplified *in praesentia*. (My use of the term 'behaviour' in this context is not innocent; Freud describes transference as an action). Given these basic concepts, there are of course many variations on the theme of 'what to do about transference?' Should it be used? Should it be interpreted in an attempt to resolve it ? Should it be interpreted in such a way as to make it evolve? Ida MacAlpine, who is one of the most lucid analysts to have written on the topic, rightly denounces the illusory claim that it is possible to resolve transference. But whatever the practical options may be, the Freudian theoretical base remains unchanged.

Hollow transference and full transference

There are of course many questions that could be discussed here, but our task is to introduce a fundamentally new perspective based upon the seduction theory: the basis of the primal relationship with the other is one of primal seduction, and the basis of the relationship with the analyst reactivates that relationship, or even gives it an absolute sense. I will attempt to clarify this formulation by making a distinction between full and hollow transference. We can begin by stating that both hollow and full transference are established ... in a hollow. The neutrality of the analyst is one aspect of this hollow; it is probably its most superficial aspect, as it refers essentially to the fact that his features are masked, to the theory that he is a neutral mirror or a passive receiver. I would suggest that the hollow should not be interpreted solely in terms of neutrality, that it should be seen as the establishment of a relationship with someone who is supposed to know. Over and beyond the analyst's refusal to draw attention to himself in the real, we find what I have referred to as a refusing to know. Elsewhere (Laplanche, 1984) I have described this in rather different terms by speaking of the 'transcendance of transference'. And what settles in the hollow established by the analyst and his refusing to know? It may be either a plenum or a hollow. If it is a plenum, we have a positive reproduction of forms of behaviour, relationships and childhood imagos. If it is a hollow, we again have a reproduction, but this time it is the childhood relationship that is repeated; it regains its enigmatic character, and the imagos are not really full. Inevitably, full and hollow coexist alongside one another. I am therefore not saying that one is preferable to the other. I am simply stating that if full transference were all that we had, we would never be able to emerge from the plenum (the typical situation described by Freud is a full transference which reproduces archaic situations without any element of mystery). In such cases, interpretation inevitably takes the form of disavowal at some point or other: 'You are ascribing your mother's features to me' says the analyst (and the analysand readily agrees), 'but I am not your mother'. The next stage is projection: 'It isn't me who ... It's you who ...' Projection is the cross psychoanalysts have to bear; the cross of a transference which cannot be resolved.

Resolving, analysing and dissolving means slipping a knife in somewhere, and it is not possible to slip a knife in if there are no cracks, no cleavage planes. A hollow transference is a hollow which fits into another hollow. The enigmatic messages of childhood are reactivated, investigated and worked through thanks to the situation itself as it facilitates the return of the enigmatic and secondary revision. As I have already indicated, full and hollow transference are two different but complementary aspects of the same thing; but it is *only* when a split appears in the heart of the transferential imagos or scenes, only when it is possible to slip in the knife, that full transference can evolve into hollow transference and be worked through.

Psychoanalytic literature certainly contains indications that transference is not as compact as it is sometimes claimed to be. I am thinking particularly of Freud and of the insistence of the ambivalence of transference, or of Klein, who puts the accent on the depressive position, which is precisely where ambivalence comes into play. But whether we are dealing with a good object or a bad object is largely irrelevant; the important point is that splitting and the enigma can both be worked through in infantile imagos and in the relationship with the analyst.

4.3 The process

My third point concerns the *process* of analysis. Are interpretation and constructions simply means to an end? Or are they synonymous with the process itself, and are they governed by the fundamental ontological proposition which states that the human subject is a self-interpreting, self-theorizing and self-symbolizing subject? At this stage, we can do no more than outline two areas for further work.

Levels of theorization

We have to look first of all at the problem of relations between theory and practice. This problem takes on a new urgency if we say that analysis itself is a 'theorization' or a self-theorization. I place the term 'theorization' in inverted commas so as to suggest that theory can be understood in a variety of ways. At least two, and probably three, levels of theorization can be identified. Firstly, we have general theory, of which the present text is an example; general theory has to be reconstructed of the basis of new foundations and it is therefore a metapsychology. It would be absurd to claim that I intend to introduce that level of theory into practical analysis. It is not simply that theory must not intrude into analysis; it is there to limit the intrusions of any theory which is alien to the subject. At the opposite extreme, we have the subject's self-symbolization, and that is synonymous with analytic treatment itself. The distinction between interpretation and construction is probably Freud's most important contribution to this debate (Freud, 1937). Interpretation helps us to recognize certain signifiers which appear in the course of treatment, but they always appear in punctual fashion, whereas construction means that the subject really does reconstruct his own history. But the human being's self-theorization is not based on nothing; no human being and no analysand invents his life story from scratch. We do not have an infinite number of scenarios at our disposal. Between the two extremes represented by self-theorization (and analytic treatment is a privileged moment within that theorization) and the general theory of psychoanalysis, there is, then, room for an intermediary level, or for theoretical schemata which are in part bound up with a cultural milieu. I am thinking here particularly of children's theories of sexuality, of complexes and so on. I see no reason not to rehabilitate culturalism at this level. I see, for example, no reason why the Oedipus and the castration complex should not be seen as possible variations on culturally determined scenarios. And it is, of course, here that we find a place for 'primal fantasies', once we accept that these general fantasy schemata are not a phylogenetic heritage and that they do not constitute the nucleus of the unconscious.

Analysis interminable and the transference of transference

My second suggestion as to the nature of the process relates to the end of the analysis. Let me introduce three terms: 'limited', 'interminable' and 'terminated'. Analysis is limited: it is limited by the unconscious and, even within the unconscious, it is limited by what I call the source-objects of the drive. It is possible to breach this unconscious limit, and to push it back, but it is not possible to abolish it, as Freud hoped. My second proposition is that even though – or perhaps because — it is limited, analysis is also interminable. Fortunately for human beings, self-interpretation is, potentially, an infinite process. It will be a very sad day when that process comes to an end! But the fact that self-interpretation is infinite does not mean that the analytic situation is infinite or that every analysis is interminable. And it is at this point that we have to introduce a third term: the end. In the light of what has been said above, the end cannot mean the 'resolution of transference' because transference is a relationship with the enigmatic object. It may simply mean that the process of transference is transferred into one or more different sites, one or more different relationships. The transference of transference is, then, the only conceivable end for a psychoanalysis. The most difficult thing to grasp is, of course, the turning point at which it becomes possible to transfer the transference. Two images come to mind: that of a transporter bridge, and that of launching a rocket to another planet. There are limited and well-defined 'windows' in time during which it is possible to send a rocket to Saturn. Similarly, there are definite moments when it is possible to decide to end the analysis. If we miss them, we set off on a new cycle, a new twist in the spiral.

All the points that have been made here are to a large extent still in a programmatic state, and their only purpose is to show that the general theory of seduction is not (as Freud's pejorative expression would have it) merely 'the top of the structure', but something which can offer a solid basis for new developments within the practice of psychoanalysis.

Notes

1 I refer to the International Symposium on 'New Aspects of Anxiety' which took place at the Académie de Médicine on 24–26 April 1985. See the account given in *Le Monde*, 24 April 1985, p. 15.

2 I refer to this as an attack by the source-object (cf. Laplanche, 1979b).

3 Cf. ibid., p. 225: 'One must never allow oneself to be misled into applying the standards of reality to repressed psychical structures...'. If the psychoanalyst is urged not to introduce 'standards of reality', how can the 'exigencies of life' introduce them into the human unconscious?

4 When we come to discuss the seduction hypothesis, it will be seen that the function of maternal attention is eminently 'anti-homeostatic'.

5 The following passage (Freud, 1920, p. 24) is also worthy of attention:

It will be seen that there is nothing daringly new in these assumptions: we have merely adopted the view on localization held by cerebral anatomy, which locates the 'seat' of consciousness in the cerebral cortex — the outermost, enveloping layer of the organ. Cerebral anatomy has no need to consider why, anatomically, consciousness should be lodged on the surface of the brain instead of being safely housed somewhere in its inmost interior. Perhaps *we* shall be more successful in accounting for this situation in the case of our system *Pcpt.-Ps.*

6 This dialectic is inevitably overlooked by those who translate

the terms in such a way as to blur the distinction between them.

7 Which should be rebaptized the 'Aristarchean Revolution' in honour of Aristarches of Samos.

8 I will not enter into a detailed discussion of the basic differences between Darwinism and Lamarckianism. Suffice it to say that both deny the possibility of the hereditary transmission (by the germ cell) of characteristics acquired in the course of either individual or collective existence (by the soma).

9 I see no reason to reject the Freudian notion of 'depth psychology' unless, of course, we fall for a snobbery which may well be no more than a survival from a *certain* phenomenology.

10 *Yau d'poele* is, according to George, the title given to members of the Lacanian 'confraternity', who allegedly greet one another with the almost meaningless phrase *'Salut, yau d'poêle'* (tr.).

11 Lacan (1975, p. 20) calls it *linguisterie* [a neologism suggesting a parody of linguistics; tr.]. Psychoanalysts have their form of *linguisterie*, but so do the linguists. There are as many schools, and as many conceptual options, as there are individuals. When it comes to hair-splitting, distinguos and exegesis, linguistics is more than a match for psychoanalysis.

12 I prefer to use the term 'apparatus of the soul' rather than 'psychical apparatus' in that it is a better index of the thesis that will be put forward later: 'psychoanalytic' is synonymous with neither the psychical in its entirety nor the psychological.

13 *Bible oblige*. But there again, if we glance at Chouraqui's attemp to retranslate the Bible, we find that 'Genesis' has disappeared and that the first book is now entitled *'Entête'* ('Heading'). A daring neologism.

14 On this basis, we can formulate a programme for the re-working of *The Intepretation of Dreams*.

15 See, for example, the theoretical section of Annie Vintner's most recent study (Vintner, 1985).

16 In a relatively late and little-known paper on the origins of transference, Klein (1952b) specifically rejects the hypothesis of a pre-object phase. My objections to Klein remain, however, intact: her failure to distinguish between self-preservation and the love−hate pair prevents her from grounding her position in either metapsychology or biology.

17 The theory that instinctual anxiety appears first is further developed in the *Introductory Lectures*, where Freud discusses the

child's fear of the dark and of strangers. Appearances are deceptive: it is in fact the anxiety occasioned by being separated from its mother that is fixated on strangers. I would simply add, drawing on Klein, that it is fixated on strangers who take on the bad aspects of the mother. Personally, I would say that the child's ego is overwhelmed because it is attacked from within by a source-object which cannot be symbolized. The anxiety occasioned by the real, or which arises when a stranger, and not the mother, enters the room, is merely a fixation of that instinctual anxiety (cf. Laplanche, 1980a, pp. 63–73; Laplanche, 1979b).

18 Or, as Roy Schafer (1976) would no doubt say in his terminological crusade against the use of substantives, 'something unconsciously'.

19 The initial situation is described without reference to the theory of the unconscious in the hope that the description will lead us to the theory, as defined in a more realist and topographical sense. Cf. the afterword to chapter 3.

20 The question of the 'infinite reference back' cannot be resolved either by adopting a 'realist' position or by investigating the fantasm. In both cases the analysand is confronted with a supposedly conclusive revelation ('And there you have it') and is quite entitled to say 'So what'.

21 Cf. Spinoza (1677):

Definition II: I say that we act or are active when something takes place within us or outside of us whose adquate cause we are, that is, when from our nature anything follows in us or outside us which can be clearly and directly understood through that alone. On the other hand, I say that we suffer or are passive when something takes place in us or follows from our nature of which we are only the partial cause. Proposition I: Our mind acts certain things and suffers others: namely, in so far as it has adequate ideas, and in so far as it has inadequate ideas, thus far it necessarily suffers certain things.

22 It should again be noted that evolution of theory (the transition from ego as individual to ego as agency) corresponds to a development movement which occurs in the real, in the genesis of the psychical apparatus of the human being.

Bibliography

Anzieu, Didier (1985) *Le Moi-peau*, Paris: Dunod.
—— (1986) *Une Peau pour les pensees*, Paris: Clancier-Guenaud.
Balint, Michael (1937) 'Early Developmental States of the Ego. Primary object-Love'. In *Primary Love and Psychoanalytic Technique*, London: The Hogarth Press and the Institute of Psychoanalysis (1959).
Balmary, Marie (1979) *L'Homme aux statues. Freud et la faute cachée du Père*, Paris: Grasset.
Bleichmar, Silvia (1985) *Aux Origines du suject psychique dans la clinique psychanalytique de l'enfant*, Paris: PUF.
Ey, Henri and Rouart, Julien (1938) *Essai d'application des principes de Jackson à une conception dynamique de la neuropsychiatrie*, Paris: Monographie de *L'Encephale*.
Federn, Paul (1952) *Ego Psychology and the Psychoses*, New York: Basic Books.
Ferenczi, Sandor (1926) 'The Problem of the Acceptance of Unpleasant Ideas — Advances in the Knowledge of the Sense of Reality'. In *Further Contributions to the Problems and Methods of Psychoanalysis*, London: The Hogarth Press and the Institute of Psychoanalysis (1926).
—— (1933) 'Confusion of Tongue between Adults and the Child'. In *Final Contributions to the Problems and Methods of Psychoanalysis*, London: The Hogarth Press and the Institute of Psychoanalysis (1955).
Freud, Sigmund, *The Standard Edition of the Complete Psychological Works of Sigmund Freud* (24 vols), London: The Hogarth Press and the Institute of Psychoanalysis (1953—73). (Hereafter referred to as SE.)
—— (1896a) 'Further Remarks on the Neuro-Psychoses of Defence', SE III.

—— (1896b) 'The Aetiology of Hysteria', SE III.

—— (1900) *The Interpretation of Dreams*, SE IV–V.

—— (1905) *Three Essays on the Theory of Sexuality*, SE VII.

—— (1908) 'On The Sexual Theories of Children', SE IX.

—— (1910a) 'Leonardo da Vinci and a Memory of his Childhood', SE IX.

—— (1910b) 'The Psychoanalytic View of Psychogenic Disturbance of Vision', SE XI.

—— (1911a) 'Formulations on the Two Principles of Mental Functioning', SE XII.

—— (1911b) 'Psychoanalytic Notes on an Autobiographical Account of a Case of Paranoia (Dementia Paranoides)', SE XII.

—— (1912-13) *Totem and Taboo*, SE XIII.

—— (1913) 'The Claims of Psychoanalysis to Scientific Interest', SE XIII.

—— (1914) 'On Narcissism: An Introduction', SE XIV.

—— (1915a) 'Instincts and their Vicissitudes', SE XIV.

—— (1915b) 'The Unconscious', SE XIV.

—— (1916-17) *Introductory Lectures on Psychoanalysis*, SE XV–XVI.

—— (1917) 'A Metapsychological Supplement to the Theory of Dreams,' SE XIV.

—— (1918a) 'The Taboo of Virginity (Contributions to the Psychology of Love II), SE XI.

—— (1918b) 'From the History of an Infantile Neurosis', SE XVII.

—— (1920) *Beyond the Pleasure Principle*, SE XVIII.

—— (1923) *The Ego and the Id*, SE XIX.

—— (1926a) 'Inhibitions, Symptoms and Anxiety' SE XX.

—— (1926b) 'The Question of Lay Analysis', SE XX.

—— (1933) *New Introductory Lectures on Psychoanalysis*, SE XXII.

—— (1937) 'Constructions in Analysis', SE XXIII.

—— (1938) *An Outline of Psychoanalysis*, SE XXIII.

—— (1939) *Moses and Monotheism*, SE XXIII.

—— (1950) *A Project for a Scientific Psychology*, SE I.

—— (1985) *The complete Letters of Sigmund Freud to Wilhelm Fliess 1887–1904*, Jeffrey Moussaief Masson (tr. and ed.), Cambridge Mass. and London: The Belknap Press of Harvard University Press.

—— (1987) *A Phylogenetic Fantasy. Overview of the Transference Neuroses*, Cambridge, Mass.: The Belknap Press of Harvard University Press.

George, François (1979) *L'Effet 'Yau de poêle'*, Paris: Hachette.

Green, André (1979), 'L'Enfant Modèle', *Nouvelle Revue de Psychanalyse*, 19, Spring.

Grinstein, Alexander (1956—71) *The Index of Psychoanalytic Writings*, (14 vols), New York: International Universities Press.

Groddeck, George (1935) *The Book of the It. Psychoanalytic Letters to a Friend*, London: The C.W. Daniel Company.

Heimann, Paula (1952) 'Certain Functions of Introjection and Projection in Early Infancy'. In Melanie Klein et al.,*Developments in Psychoanalysis*, London: The Hogarth Press and the Institute of Psychoanalysis (1952).

Jones, Ernest (1954) *Sigmund Freud: Life and Work. Vol I : The Formative Years and the Great Discoveries, 1865—1900*, London: The Hogarth Press.

Juranville, A. (1984) *Lacan et la philosophie*, Paris: PUF.

Kant, Immanuel (1785) *Fundamental Principles of the Metaphysics of Morals*, Thomas K. Abbot (tr.), Indianapolis and New York: Bobbs-Merril (1949).

Klein, Melanie (1952a) 'On Observing the Behaviour of Young Infants'. In Melanie Klein et al., *Developments in Psychoanalysis*, London: The Hogarth Press and the Institute of Psychoanalysis 1952).

——— (1952b) 'The Origins of Transference'. In *The Writings of Melanie Klein: Vol III. Envy and Gratitude and Other Works, 1946—1963*, London: The Hogarth Press and the Institute of Psychoanalysis (1975).

Klein, Melanie, Heimann, Paula, Isaacs, Susan and Riviere, Jean (1952) *Developments in Psychoanalysis*, London: The Hogarth Press and the Institute of Psychoanalysis (1952).

Kossack, M. (1913) 'Sexuelle Verführung der kinderdurch Dienstboten', *Sexual Probleme*, January.

Krüll, Marianne (1986), *Freud and his Father*, Arnold J. Pomerans (tr.), London: Hutchinson.

Lacan, Jacques (1949) 'The Mirror Stage as Formative of the Function of the I'. In *Ecrits; A Selection*, Alan Sheridan (tr.), London: Tavistock (1977).

——— (1955) 'Variantes de la cure-type'. In *Ecrits*, Paris: Seuil (1966).

——— (1975) *Le Séminaire. Livre XX: Encore*, Paris: Seuil.

——— (1977) *The Four Fundamental Concepts of Psychoanalysis*, Alan

Sheridan (tr.), London: The Hogarth Press and the Institute of Psychoanalysis.

Lagache, Daniel (1950) 'Le Problème du transfert'. In *Oeuvres III: Le Transfert et autres travaux psychanalytiques*, Paris: PUF.

—— (1961) 'La Psychanalyse et la structure de la personnalité'. In *Oeuvres IV: Aggressivité, structure de la personnalité et autres travaux*, Paris: PUF.

Laplanche, Jean (1976) *Life and Death in Psychoanalysis*, Jeffrey Mehlmann (tr.), Baltimore: Johns Hopkins Press (1st edn 1970).

—— (1979a) 'Le Structuralisme devant la psychanalyse', *Psychanalyse à l'université*, 4, 15.

—— (1979b) 'Une Métapsychologie à l'épreuve de l'angoisse', *Psychanalyse à l'université*, 4, 16.

—— (1980a) *Problématiques I: L'Angoisse*, Paris: PUF.

—— (1980b) *Problématiques II: Castration-Symbolisations*, Paris: PUF.

—— (1980c) *Problématiques III: La Sublimation*, Paris: PUF.

—— (1981) *Problématiques IV: l'Inconscient et le ça*, Paris: PUF.

—— (1984) 'Transcendance du transfert', *Psychanalyse à l'université*, 9, 35–6.

—— (1985) 'La Pulsion et son objet-source: son destin dans le transfert'. In ΛFP, *La Pulsion, pour quoi faire*, Paris: AFP (1985).

—— (1986) 'Traumatisme, transfert et autres trans(es)', *Psychanalyse à l'université*, 11, 41.

—— (1987) *Problématiques V: Le Baquet. Transcendance du transfert*, Paris: PUF.

Laplanche, Jean and Leclaire, Serge (1972) 'The Unconscious: A Psychoanalytic Study', P. Coleman (tr.), *Yale French Studies*, 48 (first published 1961).

Laplanche, Jean and Pontalis, J.B. (1968) 'Fantasy and the Origins of Sexuality', *International Journal of Psychoanalysis*, 49 (first published 1964).

—— (1973) *The Language of Psychoanalysis*, Donald Nicholson-Smith (tr.), London: The Hogarth Press and the Institute of Psychoanalysis (1st edn 1967).

Leibniz, Baron Gottfried Wilhelm Von (1714) 'Monadology'. In *Basic Writings*, George R. Montgomery (tr.), La Salle, Ill.: Open Court (1968).

MacAlpine, Ida (1950) 'The Development of the Transference', *Psychoanalytic Quarterly*, XIX.

Malcolm, Janet (1984) *In The Freud Archives*, London: Jonathan Cape.

Masson, Jeffrey Moussaief (1984) *The Assault on Truth. Freud's Suppression of the Seduction Theory*, New York: Farrar Strauss Giroux.

Mead, Margaret (1950) *Male and Female*, London: Victor Gollancz Ltd.

Merleau-Ponty, Maurice (1964) 'Maurice Merleau-Ponty à la Sorbonne. Résumé de ses cours établi par des étudiants et approuvé par lui-même', *Bulletin de psychologie*, No 236, tome XVII, 3–6.

Politzer, Georges (1928) *Critique des fondements de la psychologie*, Paris: Rieder.

Riviere, Joan (1952) 'General Introduction'. In Klein et al., *Developments in Psychoanalysis*, London: The Hogarth Press and the Institute of Psychoanalysis (1952).

Schafer, Roy (1976) *A New Language for Psychoanalysis*, New Haven: Yale University Press.

Schusdck, A. (1966) 'Freud's "Seduction Theory": A Reconstruction', *Journal of the History of Behavioural Science*, 5.

Schwartz, B.E. and Ruggieri, B.A. (1959) 'Sadism, Seduction and Sexual Deviation', *Medical Times*,87.

—— (1975) 'Morbid Parent–Child Passions in Delinquency', *Social Therapy*, 3

Sperber, Hans (1912) 'Ueber den einfus sexueller Momente auf Entstehung und Entwicklung der Sprache', *Imago*, I.

Spinoza, Baruch (1677) 'Ethics'. In *Spinoza's Ethics and De Intellectu Emendatione*, A. Boyle (tr.), London: Everyman (1910).

Stein, Conrad (1986) 'Qu'est-ce qu'on t'a fait, à toi, pauvre enfant?', *Psychanalyse à l'université*, II, 42, 43.

—— (1987) 'De la séduction en Psychologie: Journées d'études freudiennes, octobre 1986', *Etudes freudiennes*, 29.

Vichyn, B. (1984) 'Naissance des concepts: auto-érotisme et narcissisme', *Psychanalyse à l'université*, 9, 36.

Vintner, Annie (1985) *L'Imitation chez le nouveau-né*, Neuchatel and Paris: Delachaux and Niestlé.

Winnicott, D.W. (1953) 'Transitional Objects and Transitional Phenomena'. In *Collected Papers: Through Paediatrics to Psychoanalysis*, London: Tavistock Publications (1958).

Index